GIVING A
CHEESE & WINE
TASTING PARTY

GIVING A
CHEESE & WINE
TASTING PARTY

BY BETTY WASON

PUBLISHERS · GROSSET & DUNLAP · NEW YORK

ACKNOWLEDGMENTS

The author wishes to thank the following for their courtesy in granting permission to use their illustrations, which include sketches of grapes by Walter S. Taylor, the Greek Amphora provided by Sebastiani Vineyards, and wine labels from many sources. Following are the pages on which the illustrations appear: Peter Aaron, 43, 44, 45, 49 *(top)*, 89; Almadén Vineyards, 23 *(left)*, 26; Baccarat Crystal, 33; Borden Foods Division, Borden, Inc., 65, 86; Bully Hill Vineyards, Inc., 20 *(top)*; Champagne News & Information Bureau, 13 *(bottom)*, 30, 31, 32, 33; The Christian Brothers, 37; Dairylea Cooperative Inc., 59, 60; N. Dorman & Co., Inc., 61, 62 *(bottom)*, 63; Food and Wines from France, Inc., 14, 62 *(top)*, 71 *(bottom)*; E. & J. Gallo Winery labels, 39, 40 *(top)*; German Wine Information Bureau, 46, 47; Gold Seal Vineyards, Inc., 38; Heublein, Inc., 50; The House of Cinzano, label, 48; The House of Ruffino, labels, 48; Kraft Foods, 11, 64, 71 *(top)*; Charles Krug Winery, 36, 53 *(top)*; Libbey Glass, 82, 83, 84; Paul Masson Vineyards, 17, 18, 34 *(bottom)*; Sebastiani Vineyards, 13, 39 *(top)*, 52; The Sherry Institute of Spain, 27, 28, 29; Greyton H. Taylor Wine Museum, 15, 22, 46 *(top)*; The Taylor Wine Company, Inc., 21 *(bottom)*, 22, 24, 25; United Dairy Industry Association, 57; United Vintners, Inc., 35, 41 *(bottom)*, 42 *(top)*; Widmer's Wine Cellars, Inc., 54, 55; Wine Institute, 9, 10, 12, 19, 23 *(right)*, 34, 36, 40, 41, 42, 49, 51, 53, 56, 67, 69, 85, 87; Wisconsin Dairies Cooperative, 73, 75, 76, 77, 78.

OTHER BOOKS BY BETTY WASON
Cooks, Gluttons, & Gourmets
The Art of Spanish Cooking
Bride In the Kitchen
The Art of German Cooking
A Salute to Cheese
Cooking to Please Finicky Kids
Low Calorie Hors d'Oeuvres Cook Book
The Everything Cook Book
Mediterranean Cook Book

Library of Congress catalog card number: 74-18875
ISBN 0-448-11903-X

First printing
Printed in the United States of America

CONTENTS

PREFACE

Most of my knowledge of wines comes from having been a wine drinker for all my adult life and having lived for a total of approximately eight years in Europe, where I became so accustomed to having wine with dinner every night, regardless, that now a dinner without wine seems incomplete to me. This is why I emphasize again and again that the best way to learn about wine is to drink it.

I have also, however, visited a number of wineries, both in this country and in Europe, and as I walked through, with that intoxicatingly beautiful fragrance filling the air, had the technique of wine making explained to me. There's nothing like visiting a winery to make one appreciate how much skill and intricate knowledge go into each step of wine making.

My personal tastes, I must confess, have been conditioned by years of drinking European wines, but when I returned to this country after five years in Portugal, I was astounded to learn of the enormous strides that had been made in the American wine industry during that time, and what truly beautiful wines are now being produced here.

To become acquainted with the flood of new American wines now available required considerable research and tasting. Leon Adams' fine book, *The Wines of America*, has been of inestimable help. So have tips from a number of wine connoisseurs I have been fortunate enough to meet in the Washington, D.C., area and who gave generously of their time in explaining which of the American wines they had found to be most outstanding. This included many of the individuals associated with Masters of Wine and Les Amis du Vin, as well as columnists and other wine writers. The city of Washington, it might be added, is considered among the most discriminating wine markets in the nation, and a wider selection of both imported and American wines and cheeses are available here than in almost any other locality.

I had previously visited California's Napa Valley and been entertained by Brother Timothy at Christian Brothers, but in the summer of 1974 I returned for a four-day tour of the wine country, in the company of Marjorie Lumm of the Wine Institute. On this trip I not only visited many more wineries but had the opportunity of interviewing both wine masters and directors at a number of the more prestigious cellars.

As for cheese, I thought I had done all the research necessary when I wrote my book *A Salute to Cheese*, but after an examination of the many wine and cheese shops that have sprung up like toadstools after rain in recent years, I realized that many of what once were rare and exotic cheeses to most Americans are now popular and fast-selling items, and that many more are now available. I am grateful to Tony Batista of the Calvert Wine Cheeserie in Washington for having brought to my attention several cheeses with which I had not previously been familiar; also to Carlos Estrada of the Georgetown Wine and Cheese Shop; and in Arlington, Colette Arntson, manager of the Cheese and Bottle Shop.

In this book I have deliberately used brand names to identify both cheeses and wines because, as I have carefully explained, there is such wide variance in products with the same type, regional, or varietal name. Outside the larger metropolitan cities, many of these will be unavailable, and it may take considerable searching to find them even in sophisticated urban areas. Therefore, where company names have been given, consider these only suggestions, and make substitutions accordingly.

Incidentally, let me say that throughout this book I use the word "host" without gender. Why shouldn't a woman be a host as much as a man? We don't refer to "doctoress" or "lawyeress," or even "authoress," so can't we dispense with "hostess" as well? And certainly female hosts are every bit as much interested in learning about wines and cheeses these days as are the male of the species!

B. W.

Wine and cheese are such natural partners you could say theirs is a marriage made in heaven. The two have much, much in common. Both are at the same time the most simple, yet the most complex of all forms of sustenance. Both are "living" products whose yeasts or enzymes cause them to continue to ripen and mature, even changing personality, as they lie stored in cave, cellar, or climate-controlled storeroom. (This is true, at least, of natural cheeses and unpasteurized wines.)

The origin of each is so old as to be shrouded in legend. No one knows for a certainty who first discovered that the bubbling fermentation of grapes lying in a trough or vat created a beverage that could lighten men's hearts and make life seem more joyous. Nor does anyone really know who first learned that the pressed curds of milk left in a cave could develop into a solid food with enticingly piquant flavor.

Poets and philosophers have lauded the virtues of cheese and wine from time immemorial. Cheese molds have been discovered in ancient rubble dating back to more than a thousand years before the birth of Christ, and pictures on the walls of Egyptian tombs prove that the art of viticulture was carried on four thousand years ago with methods not unlike those still in use today.

Yet every year in this, our own century, new cheeses are "invented," new wines brought forth. It would be impossible for any one person, even a professional taster, to be familiar with them all.

THE BEST KIND OF PARTY

Traminer grapes, grown in the cooler regions of California, particularly Sonoma and the Napa Valley.

This is why both cheese and wine lore are so fascinating. The most jaded gourmet can always learn something new. And there is, as well, the endless provocation of comparative tasting. Can the sample of Brie for sale in a suburban specialty shop bear comparison with that superb, runny-soft Brie one enjoyed last summer in Paris? And what about the various California wines carrying the varietal name Cabernet Sauvignon on their labels—which has the most velvety texture, the most persuasive bouquet? And why should one or two of the lot, from the same region in the same vintage year, measure up so much better than the others?

Within just the last decade, suddenly Americans want to know everything about wine. It could almost be called a cultural explosion.

Even in families who never before kept wine in their homes, serving wine to guests has become *de rigeur*. Every year more American farmland is planted in vineyards: twice as many new vineyards were established in 1973 as in the previous year, and in widely scattered parts of the country. Now in forty-four out of fifty states, vineyards produce wine grapes. Wine sales have doubled, tripled, in localities deep in the hinterland: in 1971, wine sales rose 59 percent in Wisconsin, 65 percent in Vermont, 89 percent in Rhode Island.

The number of Americans making wine in their homes has so increased that virtually all large department stores sell home winemaking kits, and the amateur enologists may order juice and special wine yeasts not simply for plain red, white, or rosé wines, but for such varietals as Zinfandel, Barbera, Pinot Blanc, or one of the new French hybrids. It's estimated that, at certain times of the year in at least a quarter of a million American homes, vats can be heard bubbling as wine ferments in basement or closets.

The word "wine" has long had a connotation of romantic wickedness, but what America's young lovers are presently learning is that wine lore is so fascinating that an evening devoted to tasting different wines, a sip at a time, while seriously discussing the bouquet and flavor of one wine as compared to another, can be the greatest fun.

The discovery of lovely new taste sensations is only part of it. Wine has a subtle effect; it provokes thoughtful and sparkling conversation, so different from the raucous noise of a cocktail party. And not least of the attractions of a wine tasting is the kind of people it brings together. For people who are wine lovers share a zest for living, an avid curiosity, and a desire to embrace joy.

For generations, wine tastings were put on only for the buyers, the professionals who sniffed and sipped critically at the samples placed before them as a way of selecting the best for the market. Then some slick PR man conceived of this as a way of introducing the great variety of wines to a public that knew virtually nothing about the beverage, even looked upon it as a snob's drink. Suddenly, what had begun as a strictly commercial form of promotion, a means of persuading more Americans to buy wine, achieved a success that surprised even the promoters.

Without doubt, timing was a big factor in bringing about this extraordinary change in attitude. Americans returning from overseas during and after World War II brought back a taste for the exotic in both food and drink. Then tourism in the affluent sixties took the trend a step forward. Putting a bottle of wine on the dinner table became that extra something, that touch of elegance which could dress up the plainest menu.

But at first even those who knew what to ask for had a hard time finding a decent selection of wines in American liquor stores. The men behind the counter couldn't care less: there was a much bigger profit in booze, so why bother with wine?

Public wine tastings changed all that. Americans who had never left our native shores began to come into shops asking for such strange-sounding products as Pouilly-Fumé, Beaujolais, or Schwarze Katz. Finally the smarter liquor dealers could see they had better stock their shelves with a larger selection of wines, domestic and imported, if they wanted their more sophisticated customers to keep coming back.

During this time, California surged way ahead of the rest of the nation in the matter of wines. Not only does California produce 85 per-

California is able to produce vast quantities of wine due to its broad range of climate, ideal for growing many different varieties of grapes.

cent of all American wines, but as in all regions where wine is plentiful and cheap, the vintner's output is looked upon as an everyday beverage, not a luxury. Visiting the more than two hundred California wineries that have public tasting rooms has become a favorite weekend occupation for Californians, who drink twice as much wine per capita as the rest of the country put together.

Today Californians approach wine drinking quite as seriously as the French, exchanging news about upcoming wineries and especially fine varietals, buying wines with good aging qualities directly from the vintners and storing them away in their own cellars. Apartment managers in San Francisco even make individual "wine caves" available to their tenants, deep in basements away from heat.

It was in California that the custom of giving private wine tastings first began, as the best way of making comparative taste tests. The vast selection of wines available in shops now is so overwhelming, how can the beginner know which to buy? And not only beginners! Dedicated connoisseurs have a hard time keeping up with the premium wines being produced by the dozens, of truly outstanding small wineries that have sprouted up in the last decade. Multiply this vast assortment of American wines by those coming from other countries—and not only table wines, but fortified wines, sparkling wines, and dessert or after-dinner wines—and the consumer is frankly overwhelmed.

Interest in gourmet cheeses has kept pace with this contagious fascination with wine, and for much the same reason. A quarter century ago, dairy shelves in the typical grocery or supermarket carried little else but the plastic-wrapped process cheeses of rubbery texture and bland flavor useful for lunchbox sandwiches but rarely provocative of ecstatic praise.

Today every metropolitan American city has its cheese shops, offering a selection of hundreds of cheeses from around the world,

Five varieties of cheese offer a tempting and attractive snack or party fare: from left, Cracker Barrel, Colby (tower), Swiss, Gouda spread and Muenster sticks.

plus a continuously expanding line of fine American cheeses of every shape, texture, and type. As in viniculture, so in cheese production: the tendency has been to copy European types and to give American originals European names. But as appreciation of cheese varieties grows, more and more domestic cheese manufacturers are daring to give their own names to their own superb products.

Copy of a full-color poster painted for the Wine Advisory Board by San Francisco artist Amadeo Gonzalez.

Recognizing the natural partnership of wine and cheese, today, in many American cities, shops sell and promote the two together, and not infrequently such wine and cheese shops advertise the services of a party consultant to assist customers who want help in selecting a menu for a tasting or party.

Making up a menu of nothing else but wine and cheese is indeed an easy way to entertain. One doesn't have to do a single bit of cooking, even if as many as fifty or sixty guests are coming. Just put out the cheese, bread, and wafers, the bottles of wine and glasses enough to go around, and let host and guests enjoy themselves together.

But wait—whether or not such a party will go over depends largely on the guests. To give a "tasting" as a substitute for a cocktail party is absurd. People who still know very little about wine, and whose acquaintance with cheese is still largely limited to the processed varieties, are not going to be all that intrigued. They may be impressed by the sight of such exotic fare, but inwardly they'd just as soon be offered highballs or a punch and spicy hors d'oeuvres.

This does not mean, however, that wine and cheese should not be paired together as the basis for a big-party menu. But distinguish between a "tasting" and a "party." If you are inviting friends whom you know are seriously interested in improving their gastronomic education, keep the gathering small. Somewhere between five and twenty guests, no more.

On the other hand, if you are inviting people whose tastes are not so sophisticated, or perhaps simply people who are acquaintances rather than friends (what I shall refer to from now on as a "mixed group"), you needn't offer more than four kinds of wine, or four to six kinds of cheese, and the latter may include cheese spreads, a fondue, hot cheese balls, and other hors d'oeuvres.

Even in making the selection for such a party, you need to know wines and cheeses yourself. And the best way of doing this is first to have a number of private tastings, small tastings, in the company of close friends.

In fact, the only way to learn about wine is to drink it, fairly often, in moderate amounts, until your palate begins to detect instantly the difference between wines.

Similarly, the best way to become knowledgeable about fine cheeses is to eat them, as snacks or desserts, frequently enough to be familiar with some at least of that long list of cheeses on the "bulletin board" of your favorite cheese shop. Then, as a host, you, too, will enjoy yourself a great deal more.

As you sip at a glass of wine, you may appreciate the subtlety of this provocative drink more if you are aware of its fascinating history, of the long and careful process that goes into its cultivation, and if you know why wines can vary so enormously one from another.

Wine should never be downed quickly to produce a "high," or as a simple thirst quencher, like water. On the contrary, each wine, measured sip by thoughtful sip, with the same sort of meditative observation as the art lover bestows on paintings in a museum, should be enjoyed as much for its particular taste and fragrance as for that relaxing warmth it sends through your veins.

THE EARLIEST VINTNERS

Even the cavemen seem to have been vintners of a sort, judging by the remnants of wine dregs in the shards of earthenware cups found in the oldest of prehistoric sites. And what was the first thing Noah did when he returned home after the Great Flood? He became a husbandman and planted a vineyard. But the wine on which Noah became so disgracefully drunk that he fell asleep naked in his tent probably bore little resemblance to the beverages we call by that name today. More likely, like the caveman's drink, it was thick with sediment and still so young as to be raw and dyspeptic.

Yet the art or science of viticulture is more than twenty-six hundred years old, for it was about the year 700 B.C. that the Greek poet Hesiod wrote a treatise on the subject, drawing on his own experiences and observations as to what elements helped to produce superior wines.

Why have grapes rather than other fruits been so extensively used in wine making? Because a microscopic enzyme existing on the skins of all grapes causes fermentation within a brief time after the juice has been pressed from the grapes. In fact, it's safe to assume that the first wine made itself, when juice oozing out from overripe grapes in a basket began to ferment.

This grape fermentation often has an uncanny wildness about it. As the pressed juice—the "must," as it is called—lies in the vat, the liquid begins to seethe and bubble, and a loud buzzing like a horde of angry bees may be heard. It does indeed seem that a ghostly spirit, or at least a mischievous gremlin, has stirred up that tumult.

Today wine makers carefully control and guide the fermentation according to the type of wine being produced, and add fresh yeast spores rather than depending on the capriciousness of enzymes on the grape skins. Fermentation is controlled by temperature, and scientific machinery has replaced the foot and handwork that once served as a ritual marking each step of the mysterious conversion of grapes into wine. Yet basically wine is made according to the same principles, and with many of the same techniques, used in Hesiod's day.

The Greeks of antiquity knew, as vintners still recognize, that the most important elements in wine making are Nature's own contribution: the particular qualities of the grapes themselves, the soil where the vines are planted, the slope of the hillside, the amount of sun the soil catches and reflects during the growing season, whether the rains come in their proper time, and if the grapes are permitted by the weather to ripen to the point where they have just the desired amount of natural sugar. It isn't simply a question of finding fertile soil; on the contrary, soil that is primarily slate, chalk, or gravel,

LEARNING ABOUT WINE

Fired clay Amphorae, made by the Greeks, are known to have been used to transport and store wine at least fifteen centuries before Christ. Entire cargoes of these ancient Grecian jars have been found on the bottom of the Mediterranean Sea, some still containing wine.

Thousands of years separate the Greek amphora from these early Champagne bottles, probably used in the 18th and 19th centuries.

where other fruits and vegetables could not thrive at all, may be perfect. And the manner in which the vines are pruned and cultivated also helps to determine the character of each wine, techniques Hesiod discussed in his treatise of so many years ago.

In antiquity as now, great vintage years were recognized and celebrated, and the wines of outstanding vintages sold at a far higher price than ordinary wines. Fragments of wine amphorae found at the bottom of the Mediterranean prove this: the earthenware jars bear not only the names of the wine region of origin, but the time of vintage, expressed according to the ruler then in power. Some of the ancient wines were said to possess extraordinary keeping qualities, being at their prime when twenty-five, thirty, or fifty years old.

Most renowned of them all was Pramnian, the favorite wine of the Trojan hero Nestor, and also of the enchantress Circe, who used it as the basis of the potion she offered to Ulysses' sailors—so powerful that, when they had drunk it, it turned them into swine!

Most of these ancient Greek wines seem to have been sweet and thick with sediment; the technique of racking wines to clarify them apparently had not yet been introduced. As the wines aged in their great earthenware amphorae, evaporation caused them to become thicker and sweeter, until after forty or fifty years some were like syrup. This may explain why the Greeks invariably diluted their wines with water, adding anywhere from three to twenty parts of water to one of wine. Yet even when so diluted, fine wines inspired extravagant praise.

It was the Greeks who first introduced viticulture to all other parts of the Mediterranean, and after the Greeks, the Romans carried on the tradition, planting vineyards wherever they established colonies, as far north as the Rhineland and even Britain.

One of the most renowned of Roman wines was Falernian, which, produced on volcanic slopes near Naples, was said to be still fragrantly intoxicating when one hundred years old. Pliny reported that it was the only wine that would catch fire when lighted, causing some wine historians to wonder if it might have been in fact a brandy. Galen, the Greek physician of the second century B.C., declared that Falernian was not fit to drink until it was ten years old, was at its best between fifteen and twenty years, and after that was likely to give one a headache.

Yet while some of these Roman and Greek wines lived to such a legendary age, it seems that the vintners of antiquity had plenty of problems in preserving simple, everyday wines.

The Roman agriculturist Columella included numerous techniques for preserving wine in his book, *De re rustica*, written during the first century A.D. A little seawater might be added, or liquid resin mixed with ash, and if too sour the flavor could be disguised with herbs, spices, and honey. A recipe for sweet vermouth included in one of the oldest existing cookery books, that of the first-century Roman gourmet Apicius, fits this description. Cheap wines were also sometimes "smoked" as a means of preservation: the sealed jars were placed in a loft above the *fumarium*, or smokehouse, a technique that was to be applied centuries afterward in the making of Madeira wines.

A Burgundy from the Côte de Beaune vineyards in Burgundy, complemented by a mouth-watering selection of French cheeses—soft-ripened, semisoft, processed, and goat cheeses.

Wines in that time were always stored in earthenware jars or wooden casks. Not until the latter part of the eighteenth century, only yesterday in wine's long history, would wine be bottled in glass.

THE EMERGENCE OF THE FRENCH AS MASTERS OF VITICULTURE

When Caesar's Roman legionnaires reached the hill country of the Burgondes in what is now France, they found the slopes flourishing with grapes that proved to make an extraordinarily fine wine. The origin of the Burgundy wine industry can, then, be traced back to this time. After the collapse of the Roman Empire, wine making was carried on principally by monks in the great monasteries in the region, and the wines they produced became so famous, and brought the monasteries so much wealth, that local feudal lords entered the competition, ordering large areas of their holdings plowed up to be planted in vineyards. The best of these came to be known as "château wines," each bearing the name of the château (castle) of the lord on whose estate it was produced.

When, in 1214, France's King Philip Augustus returned to Paris flushed with his great victory at the Battle of Bouvines, it was Burgundy wine he called for to be served to his celebrating Parisians, red wine from Beaune, the ancient walled town already famous as the "capital" of that renowned wine region. The very air of Beaune was and is permeated with vinous perfume, and far beneath the cobbled streets there tunnels a honeycomb of deep cellars, which served as a treasure-house where the wines could be stored in their great oak barrels, so deep underground that the temperature never varies.

Red wines from Burgundy were most in demand, but one of the greatest of the world's white wines, Chablis, was also produced in the region from very early times, in vineyards not far north of Beaune: originally the grape variety used in making Chablis was known as the Beaunois (it is now called Chardonnay, or Pinot Chardonnay).

The French mastery of viticulture and enology (the science of wine making) was not due, however, to the grape varieties that grew there or to a better climate for wine cultivation. It was primarily because of their reverence for all things gastronomic, which even by the twelfth century was becoming a national character trait. The French worshipped the wine god as if he were a god indeed. When in the fourteenth century the papacy had headquarters in Avignon, in southern France, a particularly robust red wine of the region was named Châteauneuf-du-Pape (literally, "the new castle of the Pope") after the magnificent new papal palace, where it was imbibed appreciatively by the ecclesiastics who resided in the court. And when the papacy was about to be moved back to Rome, the monk Petrarch urged Pope Urban V to reconsider the move, declaring, "Most Holy Father, the princes of the Church esteem the wines of Provence as more rare than holy water at Rome."

Vineyards were planted throughout France, and wine drunk copiously and critically, but certain wine regions became particularly famous: after Burgundy, the Rhône valley of Provence, the Champagne

© 1969, Walter S. Taylor, Greyton H. Taylor Wine Museum

Riesling grapes, reputedly found in Germany by the Romans over one thousand years ago, have adapted well to the climates of New York State and California.

district, and the region bordering the Loire valley in the central part of the country.

Yet the wines of Bordeaux, considered by many the greatest in all the world, were scarcely known to Paris as late as the fifteenth century.

THE BRITISH ROLE IN WINE HISTORY

For three hundred years, between 1154 and 1453, the port of Bordeaux was English territory, and the finest of the wonderful wines from its surrounding vineyards ended up on English tables. The English called them "clarets," from the French word *clairet*, because the red wines were light in body and had a jewellike clarity of color.

Even after Bordeaux again became French, the British remained its best wine customers, and not until the late 1600s did the picture change. Then, during another of the recurring wars between England and France, it became unpatriotic to drink claret. An excessive tariff was placed on all French wines, and the British were urged instead to drink the wines of their wartime ally, Portugal.

Now there were and are some very fine table wines produced in Portugal, but most then did not travel well. An attempt was made to popularize the wines of the Douro region in the north, east of the city of Oporto, but as table wines these were acidic, harsh and short-lived, and, after the excellence of Bordeaux wines, found little acceptance in England.

But the wine merchants of His Majesty's Government had already learned some valuable tricks elsewhere. Since Chaucer's day, sweet wines called "sack" had been imported from Spain, the Canary Islands, and Madeira, wines made more potent by the addition of brandy, which also acted as a preservative. Thus, as the casks were bounced around in the holds of ships during what was then a two months' rough sea journey to England, the wine not only held up better, it improved.

From this experience, British wine men knew that adding a bit of brandy to the fermenting vat would stop the conversion of grape sugar into alcohol, thus retaining some of the grape's natural sweetness. Applying this technique to the Douro wines worked remarkably well. The wine the London merchants now called "port," after the city of Oporto, was still a table wine, but with more sweetness than previously. Gradually the proportion of brandy was increased, and the tart Douro wines were blended with other naturally sweet wines until at last a mellow, smooth dessert wine evolved, one that became the favorite drink of English gourmets in the eighteenth and nineteenth centuries.

As a sales device, port was sold in distinctive, flat-bottomed glass jugs made to look like earthenware jugs, even to having handles. But this shape, too, was gradually changed, until elongated glass bottles were formed that could be laid horizontally in tiers, thus saving storage space. And to prevent the wine from running out while in this position, the glass bottles were fitted with corks, which swelled when moistened with the wine, making a complete seal.

Then it was discovered that a magical change came over the wine as it lay corked in those glass bottles deep in London cellars, developing greater body and mellowness and magnificent bouquet. At the time the vintners did not understand why this should be so. Now we know it was because, when wine is stored overlong in wooden barrels or casks, enough oxygen manages to seep through the pores of the wood to activate bacteria that cause the wine to turn flat and sour. Only when protected from these bacteria in a nonporous container can the living elements in the wine that create flavor and body be permitted to develop their full potential.

In the year 1775 the first bottle of vintage port was deliberately "laid away" in glass to age. By now, English wine merchants were again regularly visiting Bordeaux, and they reported to the French the extraordinary results of aging port in sealed bottles. Twenty-two years later, in 1797, the first claret was bottled for aging in glass, and thus was born the great age of vintage wines, wines that could be put away for as long as thirty or forty years, acquiring, as they lay in the bottle, truly unforgettable mellowness and bouquet.

THE MEANING OF "VINTAGE" WINES

The vintage year of any wine is the year when the grapes are harvested. In colder regions, climate conditions vary so much from year to year that some harvests will be far better than others, and the wines of these years are therefore especially treasured. But even in wine-growing areas with a fairly stable year-round climate, certain wines from certain vineyards display marked potential.

In France, the most select wines are called *premiers crus*. The best and brightest of their class, they are given different treatment from the bulk of ordinary wines. The term "premium wines" is today used throughout the wine industry to distinguish finer wines from those of lesser quality.

Other wines with not quite the same promise, but still outstanding, the French classify as *deuxièmes* or *troisièmes crus*, and these receive the same special care and attention as the *premiers crus*. There are still others, sometimes called *mineurs crus*, farther down the line in terms of finesse, bouquet, and quality, but still with promise of great potential with bottle aging. They, too, are classed as "vintage wines."

While climatic conditions in California are not as severe as in France (they are more similar to the Mediterranean countries), California, too, has certain "great years" (1973 was one), and an increasing number of American vintners now put the year of vintage on the label.

There is more than one reason for this. Regardless of whether the vintage was outstanding or ordinary, certain wines take longer to reach their peak of maturity than others. Some are at their best when young, others must have a minimum of eighteen to twenty-four months to reach their best, and still others will not have attained their full potential until they have aged in glass five, six, or as in the heavier red wines, sometimes not for ten or twelve years. There is now a trend among the producers of premium California wines to publish lists showing which wines are likely to reach their peak over what period of bottle aging.

All the more promising wines are first stored in casks or vats for at least one, sometimes two, or even three years. During this time, the wine master watches carefully to see how they are developing, and when they reach what is called "bottle ripeness," the wine is transferred to bottles, corked tightly, and put away in a cool, deep cellar, cave, or storage vault to age and ripen for another span of years.

Dedicated wine connoisseurs soon get to know which are the outstanding vineyards and wine regions, and which vintners can be most

Portal of Paul Masson's historic old mountain winery in the Santa Cruz Mountains near Saratoga, California. This picturesque winery is 123 years old; it produces champagne, wine, and brandy.

relied on to produce superior wines, and they will happily pay more for these than for ordinary wines, whatever the year of vintage. When harvested in a "great year," the price, of course, will be higher still.

"Estate-bottled" wines are produced from vineyards within the "estate" of the winery; that is, at least 95 percent of the grapes must come from the vintner's own vineyards and be bottled under his wine master's supervision. This is important because certain vineyards produce better wines than others, and when it is known exactly from which vineyards the grapes come, quality control can be better regulated.

If the label does not proclaim the wine to be estate bottled, but does give the vintage year, it means that 95 percent of the grapes used to produce the wine were harvested that year, but they may have come from a number of different vineyards, from a cooperative serving a large area, or even from other wine regions.

But keep in mind that just because the year of vintage appears on the label, it does not necessarily mean it is a superior wine. Nor

A striking view of the Paul Masson Pinnacles Vineyards in the Salinas Valley. Each one-mile row averages five and one-half tons of grapes per harvest.

will it necessarily improve with age. On the contrary, some wines are at their best when young. Beaujolais, for example, should be drunk when no more than two or three years old. If the label shows it to be four or five years old, beware! In cases like this, knowing the vintage year as it applies to a particular wine can work in reverse, warning the buyer away (though few are the wine salesmen likely to admit this).

Even premium vintage wines may reach their peak while laid away and start going downhill. It's the custom in the great wineries to uncork aging wines periodically to see how they are doing; if they are still beautiful, they may be recorked and put back to age further.

But occasionally a promising wine of a great vintage year will start to turn sooner than expected.

Several conscientious American vintners, in particular Christian Brothers and Paul Masson, believe it is a better practice to blend wines of different vintages and from different vineyards in order to maintain standard products year after year. They claim that they can do better by combining the freshness of young wines with the headier bouquet of older wines. Their premium wines can be very good indeed, and some definitely improve with bottle aging. The beginning wine drinker may feel more secure "learning" on such wines than in trying to digest too quickly all the complicated information on vintners, vintages, grape varieties, wine regions, and so on.

But once a wine drinker has been infected with the excitement of discovering "new" and subtly different wines, he will never be the same again, for there is quite as much elation to be experienced in coming across a very fine wine (especially if it's one that your friends don't happen to know about) as in tasting an exotic new dish.

THE GREAT CROSSBREEDING BEGINS

The nineteenth century was the golden age of French vintage wines. It was then that the names of certain wine regions, their communes (what we could call townships here), and vineyards became magical to connoisseurs. The château wines of Bordeaux, including Margaux, Haut-Brion, Mouton-Rothschild, and Lafite, among others, acquired legendary reputations, as did some of the Sauternes, especially Château d'Yquem. In the Burgundy wine region, comparable fame grew around the reds of Le Corton, Clos de Vougeot, Nuits-Saint-Georges, Macon, and Chambertin. The great white wines of Burgundy include Chablis, Pouilly-Fuissé, and Montrachet. (The latter is so superlative that Rabelais once said it should be drunk kneeling with head bowed.)

While California and New York are the leaders of the American wine industry, this map illustrates the wide-ranging extent of wine production in the United States.

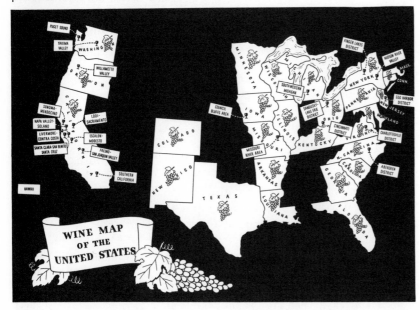

Bully Hill Vineyards, on the shore of Keuka Lake in the Finger Lakes District of New York, stand on original winery property owned by William Taylor since 1820. It is one of the finest grape-growing regions in the world.

In Germany, too, the white wines of the Mosel and Rhine valleys were making history during the same period, though this is one of the most severe climates for wine growing in the world. (Mosel, incidentally, is the German spelling, but the English and French spell it Moselle, and this is the way it is most frequently referred to in American wine publications. On bottles of wine from this area, however, you will see the spelling is Mosel.)

Midway through the nineteenth century, a little plant louse appeared that was profoundly to affect wine making throughout the world. Called the "phylloxera," this insect gnawed at the roots of vines, causing them to wither and die. Like a plague, it spread rapidly from vineyard to vineyard, crossing national boundaries and leaving many hectares of vineyard slopes ravaged and completely dead. Despite herculean efforts to deal with the insect, nothing seemed to stop it.

In the meantime, a sizable wine industry had sprung up in the United States. Ohio, Missouri, and New York State, besides California, were all producing fine table wines and champagnes. Most of the vintners were immigrants from wine-producing countries, or the sons of Old World wine makers, and many brought over with them roots of European *Vitis vinifera* wine grapes to start vineyards in the New World.

But only in certain areas would the European varieties thrive. Most American wines, at least outside of California, were produced from native grapes. Then the phylloxera crossed the Atlantic and soon was ravaging those California vineyards where *Vitis vinifera* varieties were thriving.

When it was noticed that the little louse did not bother the native American vines, vine roots from Missouri were transported to France, where, as an experiment, they were planted in French soil and then the famous *Vitis vinifera* shoots were grafted onto American roots.

Today in nearly all the world's vineyards, the wine grapes are either the product of this strange combination, American roots and European vines, or they are hybrids, made by crossbreeding European and American varieties.

Today crossbreeding is going in all directions. Many European *Vitis vinifera* grapes now thrive in American vineyards, thanks to modern research pioneered at the University of California's department of viticulture and enology at Davis. Attracting students from all over the world, this school has revolutionized the centuries-old art of viticulture by determining why certain things happen, and exactly what part climate, soil, grapes, and aging techniques play in each step of the mysterious transformation of grapes into wine. Wholly new grape varieties have been created at Davis (among them Ruby Cabernet and Emerald Riesling), particularly suited for American soil and climate conditions, but also being used by vintners in other countries.

Similar experimentation is underway in the East. Two vintners in particular, Walter S. Taylor with his Bully Hill vineyards at Hammondsport, New York, and Philip Wagner of the Boordy Vineyards in Maryland, have led the way in developing hybrid varieties, native vines crossed with European wine grapes, that will thrive and produce fine European-type wines in many different climate areas in the North and Northeast.

Philip Wagner began his crossbreeding experiments at a small family-owned winery in Maryland, but today he also has vineyards in Westfield, New York, and the Yakima Valley of Washington State.

Walter S. Taylor is a grandson of the Walter Taylor who established the great Taylor Winery in New York State, still the largest in size of any American winery outside California. But while others in the Taylor family continue to produce wines primarily from native American or *Vitis labrusca* grapes, Walter felt better wines could be produced from hybrid varieties, and today his Baco Noir red wine is regarded by connoisseurs as a truly outstanding wine.

French-born Mrs. Edmee Brooks, of the wine department at Magruder's in Washington, tells of an evening when she was entertaining a small group of European friends, connoisseurs all. First she treated them to a bottle of 1953 Château Lafite Rothschild, one of the *grands crus rouges* of Bordeaux. This was followed by a 1938 Le Corton, a rare red Burgundy whose bouquet was so magnificent that the moment the bottle was uncorked the air was permeated with its rare perfume. Then, without letting them see the label on the next bottle she opened, she served them the Bully Hill Baco Noir. Her European guests were so impressed by it they refused to believe this could be an American wine—until she showed them the label. The Bully Hill Baco Noir, made with the so-called French hybrid grapes, produced in northern New York, is now so in demand by connoisseurs it is difficult to find. Limited in production to begin with, it is quickly snapped up as soon as it appears on shelves of fine wine shops.

The chief activity at the Boordy Vineyards is in developing nursery stock rather than in wine making, and the Boordy wines cannot yet compare in quality with the Bully Hill hybrid varietals. However, the twenty or more varieties of wine grapes available from the nursery are ordered by customers from around the world—many in France, especially the Loire Valley—and by hundreds of amateur viticologists in all parts of the United States.

Even in California, growing conditions vary greatly from one area to another, even within the same county. Five climate zones have been identified by viticologists at Davis, each suitable for a particular type of wine. In fact, a climate that is sunny and warm year round is not the best for quality wine production. Some of the finest European wines come from areas with severe winters, or from vines growing high on treeless mountain slopes where wind, frost, and hail sometimes wreak cruel ravages.

A vineyard owned by The Taylor Wine Company, also on beautiful Keuka Lake.

GENERIC VS. VARIETAL WINES

The tendency in all non-European countries has been to give native wines well-known European names. Thus most red table wines have been labeled either "Burgundy," "Claret," or "Chianti," while white wines were called "Sauterne," "Chablis," or "Rhine wine," even though the wines so named often bear little resemblance to those they are intended to imitate.

These broad classifications are called "generic names." But not only is it an oversimplification to label wines this way, often the generic label is misleading. One so-called Burgundy may bear little resemblance to another, and none at all to the red wines from the Burgundy province of France. One "Rhine wine" may be quite sweet, another harshly acidic.

When the American wine industry tried to rise from the ashes of Prohibition in the 1930s, giving wines generic names seemed the easiest thing to do, but vintners who were aware of the tremendous potential of the United States as a wine-producing nation bewailed the notion that a better classification could not be established. Why not, as in Europe, name American wines for their place of origin, thus recognizing that the better American wines deserve names of their own?

The Taylor Wine Company's first building, erected in 1887. The great oval oaken doors once admitted the huge aging casks as seen on page 20.

Eventually it is almost inevitable that this will happen, and already some regional names are being used, specifically the Napa and Sonoma valleys in California and Naples Valley in New York State. Meantime, in the late 1930s, another system was introduced by the American wine expert, Frank Schoonmaker, of naming wines according to the grape variety used. Such wines are called "varietals."

The advantage of varietal names to the wine buyer is twofold: first, knowing the grape variety provides a better guide to what to expect of the wine; second, if care has been taken by the vintner to use only selected grapes, chances are good that this will be a better if not a premium wine. In fact, it can be taken as a rule of thumb that the more specific the information regarding vintage, place of origin, and grape variety given on any wine label, the more superior the wine inside the bottle is likely to be.

The disadvantage of varietal names, to the beginner at least, is that they only make wine nomenclature seem that much more complex and confusing.

How to keep all the names straight?

Maybe it's better not to try, at least not in the beginning. Just to understand what distinguishes red wine from white or rosé is a good start.

Isabella

The Isabella grape was developed in South Carolina prior to 1800, and has been grown in the Finger Lakes District since 1840. Used in the production of generic rosé wines and for blending champagnes, it is one of the native grapes classed as *labrusca*.

HOW WINE IS MADE

As important as the grape variety is to the wine, it is possible to make from one single kind of grape red, white, and rosé wines. In fact, in many a wine district, this happens every year. The color difference stems not from the grape variety, but from the length of time the grape skins remain in the fermenting vat.

When grapes are delivered to the winery, all of them are crushed in the same way (today entirely by machine), but in making white wines, the juice, or must, is promptly drawn off into a new vat before fermentation begins, separating juice from skins. If a pink, or rosé wine is wanted, the grapes, skins and all, are left in the juice for the start of fermentation, but not for very long after that. For red wines, the grapes, skin, and pips (seeds) stay in the fermenting vat throughout the period of fermentation and sometimes (for certain types of wines) for a long time afterward.

The presence of the skins during fermentation makes other differences than just color. Grape skins contain tannin, and in red wine tannin acts as a catalyst, giving the maturing wine greater body, character, and bouquet. This is why aged red wines usually have much more body and "nose" than the whites. The tannin also helps give red wines in general a longer life in the bottle than whites—though like everything else in wine lore, there are notable exceptions to this.

Periodically, new wine in the aging vat or barrel must be "racked," that is, the liquid drawn off into another vat, leaving the lees (the sediment) on the sides and bottom. These lees are scraped out and may be pressed to obtain what is called "pressed wine," which is sometimes also used in blending. (This, incidentally, is the secret of Gallo Hearty Burgundy: the straight red wine is blended with pressed wine to achieve more acidity and tannin.)

Regularly, also, more wine must be added to the vat to maintain a certain level. This is called "topping," or replenishing. The wine shrinks, from evaporation through the pores of the wooden vat, and if too much of the wine's surface is exposed to the oxygen of the air, it may turn to vinegar. The wine used for topping may be from a previous vintage or from other of the vintner's stocks, or may even be purchased from another vintner or a co-op.

Vintners once considered it essential to age all wine first in wood, and most of the "estate-bottled" and premium vintage wines still are. In fact, the choice of the kind of wood used to make the barrel or cask subtly affects the flavor of the wine.

This California vineyard is in the Livermore Valley region, southeast of San Francisco. It is most noted for its white wine grapes.

Many hundreds of gallons of wine from Almadén Vineyards are aging in these casks deep underground.

A cellarman is dwarfed by the 64,000-gallon redwood cask at the Taylor Wine Company, Hammondsport, where he is taking a sample of the wine.

Until a few years ago, the wood used in American wineries was either American oak or redwood. Then one California vintner tried using imported Limousin oak from France and found that wines aged in these casks were far more like European wines in flavor and had much more finesse. Now many of the premium California wineries use only French Limousin or Yugoslav oak, which is almost as good. The scientists, at the University of California at Davis, studying the chemical composition of American versus European varieties of oak, found that the woods are decidedly different. The use of American oak gives wines a flavor called "woody." The Limousin oak contributes a richer, fuller flavor to the wine, but the flavor is so subtle and complex it is difficult to identify; it is, however, not at all like the taste of wood.

Old redwood casks and vats are still in use in many California wineries. The largest and perhaps the oldest of all is to be seen at the Almadén winery, a huge vat that was shipped all the way to Philadelphia, via the Panama Canal, for the Centennial Exposition in Philadelphia in 1876, and shipped back to the winery afterward. But today, the manufacture of redwood wine casks is tapering off.

Increasingly, both in this country and abroad, stainless steel tanks, epoxy-lined, are being used both for the period of fermentation and (in separate vats or tanks) for aging. A considerable number of wine masters assert that the stainless steel is as suitable as wood for the making of premium wines because it is completely nonporous, lends no flavor at all to the wine, and can be thoroughly cleaned out afterward so no harmful bacteria can remain to alter future lots of wine.

The stage at which the wine is judged to be "bottle ripe" will vary from one wine to another. This is always a decision left to the wine master. Before bottling, wines are filtered, or "fined," to get rid of sediment still left in the wine; they may be fined two or three times for complete clarity.

However, some wine makers consider that further handling of the wine at this stage may disturb its fragile balance, and whatever fining takes place is done on a succession of levels, so .that the liquid will pour only downhill, with as little movement as possible.

It is because of this same fragility of the wine, the delicate balance of the esters in its complex makeup, that many experts advise letting wines "rest" several days before uncorking. Also, despite careful fining, a certain degree of sediment remains, even though so fine it cannot be seen with the naked eye. With age the sediment grows heavier, until with vintage and "crusted" ports, and also with very old Burgundies or Bordeaux, it can appear to be almost like mud in the bottom. Such sediment does not impair the flavor of the wine—it can even improve it—but it is not for drinking. For this reason, a bottle of old wine must be handled gently and the wine poured out at an angle, or better, slowly decanted into a carafe so that the sediment remains on the bottom.

The dryness or sweetness of a wine is determined to some degree during the fermentation period. When a very dry wine is wanted, the fermentation is allowed to proceed until all the natural grape sugar has been converted to alcohol. This is true of all European red table wines, but because Americans are accustomed to everything being somewhat sweetened, many of the bulk-produced red wines are deliberately blended to give them what is called "mellow" flavor, meaning a bit sweet.

White wines, even the driest, are treated quite differently. The pace of fermentation must be much slower, so the temperature of the wine inside its stainless steel vat is deliberately kept much lower than for red wines. The wine master takes the wine's temperature regularly, much as a nurse checks the fever in a patient. If the fermenting juice is allowed to become too hot, the wine will lose bouquet and may develop vinegar bacteria.

This cellarman is taking a wine sample from an oak cask, also at The Taylor Wine Company.

All, or nearly all, white wines are blends. Even when the varietal name is given on the label, only 51 percent, by law, need be from that grape variety—though a movement is growing to make this higher, as much as 85 percent. When a sweeter wine is wanted, something may be done to interrupt the fermentation before all the grape sugar has been converted. Either a little brandy may be added for a fortified wine (as already described in making port, page 16) or a bit of sulphur dioxide goes into the vat, a formula used in antiquity. Some wines will be naturally sweeter, because some grape varieties have a higher sugar content. Other varieties have a shorter growing season, permitting them to reach maximum sugar level before harvest. In some cases, grapes are deliberately left on the vines longer to develop more sugar. For very special white wines, the grapes are sometimes allowed to remain on the vines until wrinkled and oozing with syrup. If a grayish mold forms on such grapes, vintners are elated, because this mold, called *Botrytis cinerea*, gives wines a distinctive flavor and bouquet much prized by epicures. However, late-picked grapes like these must be individually selected, and such hand picking makes the wines extremely expensive.

The reason that even a varietal wine contains a small amount of wine from one or more other grape varieties is to achieve the proper balance between acidity and smoothness. Red wines, too, are blended. The famous reds of the Médoc in Bordeaux may contain as many as five grape varieties. The fact that a wine is the result of a blend does not make it inferior: it's the grapes used in the blend, the proportions used, and the manner in which they are blended that make the difference. Blending is an art that calls for both innate skill, a "feel" for the wine, and long experience. Only a wine master completely versed in the art can produce superior wines. Usually wines are blended after fermentation is complete but before the first period of aging and ripening begins.

However, when a wine is referred to as a "blended wine" in a deroga-

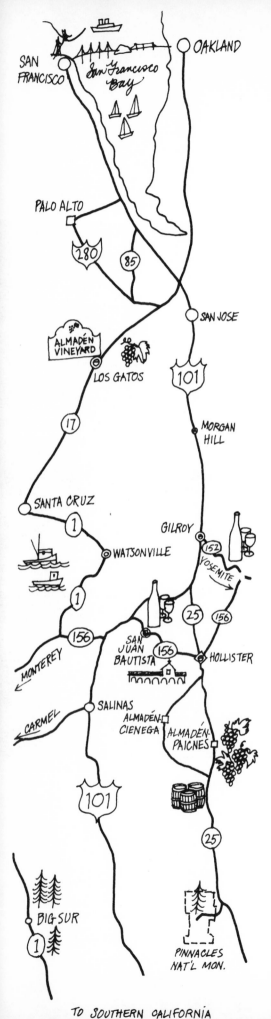

tory sense, it means it was made with grapes from many different vineyards, perhaps from different wine districts, to achieve a standardized product that can be sold at a lower price. Rarely are the better varietal grapes used in making such wines.

PASTEURIZED WINES

If the bottle or jug of table wine you buy has a metal screwcap top and no cork, you can be reasonably sure it's a pasteurized wine.

When the French chemist Louis Pasteur proved, in 1850, to a skeptical scientific world that it was bacteria from the air that caused liquids to putrefy or turn sour, he urged that his process of heating liquids to a temperature of 150 to 160 degrees Fahrenheit be used to prevent wine from going bad. At that time wine was the principal beverage drunk in French homes, as we drink water, so such an invention appeared to be of great economic benefit. But the process also killed other bacteria or microorganisms that permit a wine to develop character and potential greatness, so for this reason French vintners, proud of their reputation as the greatest masters of wine in the world, refused to adopt such a procedure.

Today, more than a century later, the process is being applied to mass-produced bulk wines, the same wines that are usually meant when the term "jug wines" is used, but among wine connoisseurs it is still regarded as a horrible practice. Even though the pasteurization takes place after the new wine is bottled, to give the wine some small chance at least of developing flavor before all the life-giving bacteria are killed, they will always remain as they were when pasteurized; they cannot develop further. They do, however, remain drinkable after opening longer than natural wines, and therefore many consider them acceptable as everyday table wines.

Recently, pasteurization has even been adopted by a group of French wine producers alarmed by a dwindling export market, to make cheap blended wines marketed under the commercial name Ecu Royale. Their French origin cannot disguise the fact that these, too, are decidedly inferior wines.

Other methods used in wine making to keep prices down and produce drinkable but dubious wines are, unfortunately, being resorted to in several countries. Sometimes the wine is diluted with water and the alcoholic content increased with straight alcohol; even coloring additives have been injected. Wines like these sometimes taste palatable enough with the first glassful, but soon after cause a headache. It is unfortunate that the growing demand for table wines has led to such corrupt practices. But it's also a reason for viewing very cheap wines with skepticism.

In many ways, pasteurized wines and pasteurized process cheese are similar. Both are standardized products with better keeping qualities under less than ideal storage conditions and are, therefore, easier to market in huge quantities. But in the process, in each case, their growth is stunted and they lose all potential for greatness.

A guide to the Almadén Vineyard sites at Los Gatos, Cienega, and Paicnes. Almadén markets sherries, California champagne, and many wines which take their names from the grape varieties used.

Why can't metal caps be used on wines that have not been pasteurized?

Again there is a mystery. The experts know what happens, but not why. One explanation given is that wine needs some oxygen to live, breathe, and ripen as it lies in the vat, but that amount must be carefully curtailed. At the stage of bottle ripeness, it must be limited still more. Glass bottles keep out all oxygen except, it is said, the infinitesimal amount that comes in through the pores of the cork. But again, I have been told, some scientists contend that almost the same amount of oxygen can seep in through the edges of the fluted metal caps.

Probably there is something in the composition of the cork, made from the bark of the cork tree, that wine likes—just as using Limousin oak instead of American oak results in wines of distinctly different flavor.

When wine that has not been pasteurized is purchased in gallon jugs or demijohns and you wish to decant it into several bottles for convenience in serving, the process must be done quickly and the bottles corked at once, not fifteen or twenty minutes later, to prevent an excess of oxygen reaching the wine. Then the bottles should be laid on their sides to keep the corks moist. For a pasteurized jug wine, such quick action is not so important, but even a pasteurized wine should not be left standing open too long, as it, too, will suffer—though to a lesser degree.

SHERRY AND OTHER "FORTIFIED" WINES

So far most of what has been said refers to table wines or light dessert wines, which usually contain less than 12 percent alcohol. A whole different class of wines are those that have been blended with brandy (like port) and range in alcoholic content from 17 percent up to 20 or 22 percent. Some of these are aperitif wines, some are best served after dinner or with dessert. Of them all, sherry was the first.

Sherry grapes drying in the blazing Spanish sun at Jerez, the birthplace of Sherry.

All Spanish Sherries are a blend of many harvests produced by a *solera* system. Sherry is stored in tiers of casks in a section of the winery *(bodega)* called the *solera*. It is from the bottom tier that the Sherry is drawn off—a limited quantity at a time—and this is replaced by younger Sherry from the tiers above. Some American vintners also use this method for their finer sherries.

Sherry labels—Fino, a pale, delicate, extra dry Sherry; served chilled, it makes an excellent aperitif. Oloroso, darker than the Fino, has a distinctive bouquet, and varies from semi-dry to very sweet; it is therefore often served as a dessert wine.

The original sherry vineyards lie on the Atlantic coast of southwestern Spain, near the town of Jerez de la Frontera, from which they get their name. These vineyards have been in cultivation for close to three thousand years, judging by wine artifacts found in the region and from references in ancient literature. A unique thing happens to these wines as they lie aging in the casks. Over some, a thick white yeast blanket forms, called the "flor." These wines, the driest sherries and (when not fortified) the lightest in alcohol, are straw colored, with an almost saline tang. The yeast blanket protects them from the microbes of the air so that they remain drinkable almost indefinitely. No such blanket forms over the rest of the wine from the harvest, even though the grapes come from the same vineyards, and no one knows what causes the difference. These other wines are called *oloroso* (a Spanish word meaning "fragrant") and are naturally somewhat sweeter, or at least, less dry.

In the tenth century, brandy was invented by Moors in that very same part of southwestern Spain. As far as is known from existing records, this was the first time in history that such a concentrated potable spirit was produced, though many centuries earlier the technique of distillation had been known and used for other purposes.

The Moors did not invent this "burnt wine," as it would be called in Germany, with any intention of drinking it. Instead, it was used as a solvent for the black eye shadow, called *kohl*, favored by ladies of the harem. Thus its original name was *al-kohl*.

What ingenious man first tried blending this brandy with the wines of Jerez, or why, is not known, but when the peripatetic British wine merchants began buying up Spanish wines for sack, always a heavily sweetened wine, someone discovered that a little brandy added to the wine helped them, as we have already mentioned, to travel more happily during the two-month sea voyage to Britain. It became the custom to blend the wines, not only with brandy, but with naturally sweeter wines made with the local Pedro Ximénes grape. Today all Spanish sherries are blends, all those for export containing brandy, and for each sherry in the great range from ultradry to very sweet a separate secret recipe, or *referencia*, is used. In what is called a *solera* system, tiers of casks are piled three or four high, and new wine is added only to the casks on the top tier, though even these already contain some wine from a previous year. In turn, after a period of aging, this newly blended wine, or part of it, is transferred to the cask beneath, aged again, and later transferred once more to the lower cask. In this way every solera sherry contains a little of the "mother wine," which may be fifty or seventy-five years old. Another characteristic of the system as followed in Spain is that the barrels are stacked above ground in roofed *bodegas* open to the air, and many believe that because the bodegas are located so close to the Atlantic coast an essence of the sea air permeates the wine through the pores of the wood, giving them that elusive, almost salty tang.

With the Spanish people, then as now, drier sherries are preferred, but for English customers in the Middle Ages, only the sweet sherries were in demand.

A story, probably apocryphal, says that in the sixteenth century, in the English port of Bristol, sherry was nicknamed "milk" because "it was the first beverage offered to infants" after the christening. One day a wine merchant offered one of his customers a taste of a new sherry he had just received. The delighted customer exclaimed, "If your other sherries are milk, this is cream, sir!" Whether the tale is true or not, it was certainly the British who gave "cream sherries" their descriptive name, and one of the best-selling of Spanish sherries of the oloroso type is known all over the world by its English name, Harvey's Bristol Cream.

After their success in blending brandy with the sherries of Spain, the British went on to try the same trick with wines from the island of Madeira, a Portuguese possession, before they tried applying it to port. When they noticed that the finest Madeiras seemed to be those which had made the long journey to India, then part of the British Empire, it was believed the rolling of the casks back and forth with the roll of the ship as it plowed through tropical seas caused that magical improvement. An attempt, then, was made to duplicate the same high temperatures and rolling movement in storage rooms called *estufas*. The temperature was gradually raised, one degree at a time, over a period of weeks, then just as gradually lowered. This same technique of "baking" wines (though not the rolling) is used by many American vintners in the production of American sherries, most of which are, in reality, more like Madeira wines than the wines of Jerez.

Later, still another brandy-blended wine was developed by British enterprise, the Marsala wine of Italy, which was intended originally to be an imitation of Spanish sherry but became renowned in its own right.

To suit differing tastes, a range of types from comparatively dry to sweet was developed, for Madeiras and ports as well as for sherries. Sercial, the driest and many consider the best of the Madeiras, is often served as an aperitif wine. It is heavier and sweeter than the driest of the sherries, more comparable to an amontillado sherry. Rainwater Madeira is a trade name, a Sercial type. Malmsey, the sweetest of the Madeiras, is made with the Malvasia grape of antiquity, brought to the Atlantic island from Greece.

The driest of the ports is white port, developed to meet today's demand for aperitif wines, but even the driest has a sweet aftertaste and little bouquet. Tawny port, a rusty reddish-brown in color, moderately sweet, and with a more persuasive "nose," remains a better seller. The finest tawny ports acquire their color with aging, beginning life as a dark red and gradually becoming lighter as they ripen. But today, even in Portugal, some of the less expensive tawnies achieve their color by having been blended. Ruby port is the least expensive and most imitated. The rarest and most superb of all are the vintage ports, made of wines from only outstanding vintage years, aged in cask for a minimum of two years, then in bottle for a minimum of twelve years. Crusted port is aged for the same length of time, but is a blend of outstanding wines from several years. The "crust" is the sediment that develops in the bottle as it ages (vintage port also has such a sediment), making it necessary that the wine be decanted before serving— the reason port is traditionally served in cut-glass decanters.

Until recently no wine called "madeira" was produced in the United States, but Paul Masson now has one. As already observed, many of the sherries, especially the cream sherries, are made by the Madeira method. American cream sherries, the better ones, manage to approximate Spanish cream sherries fairly well, but most of the American sherries called "cocktail" or "pale dry" bear little resemblance at all to the Spanish finos. Some of these make quite pleasant aperitifs, but like Marsala, they deserve a name of their own.

Señor Julio Delgado, Master Venenciador of Spain, demonstrates the ancient art of pouring Sherry with a venencia—a tiny silver cup with a three-foot long whalebone handle. Master Venenciadors earn their rank in competition between wineries. Their skill is passed from father to son for generations, one of the charming customs surrounding Sherry.

A Sherry tasting party—an old Spanish custom. *Tapas* (Spanish for hors-d'oeuvres) range from simple cubes of bread and cheese to elaborate, hot hors-d'oeuvres.

Recently, several California wineries have come up with dry sherries which are much closer to the Spanish finos, by using the imported flor yeast and following the solera system of blending and aging, then blending and aging again. Interestingly, they get better results when the flor is submerged rather than allowed to remain over the top of the wine as in Jerez. The new Almadén Flor Fino Sherry, Weibel Dry Bin Cocktail Sherry, the Paul Masson Rare Flor, and Concannon Prelude are outstanding examples.

A quite different category of brandy-fortified wines are the vermouths. These are flavored with so many herbs and spices that some wine men dismiss them contemptuously as not being wines at all.

Vermouth, the English derivation of the German word for the herb wormwood, has a history nearly as old as that of sherry. The Latin name for wormwood is *absinthium,* and a spiced herbal wine of this name was enjoyed in imperial Rome. (The absinthe blossoms are used to make vermouth; absinthe root is the base for the potent liqueur of this name favored by the French.)

"Italian" is the name often given to the sweet red vermouth, whose color is due not to the wine but to the particular flavoring ingredients that have been added, for its base is an ordinary white wine, as is that of dry, or "French," vermouth, a comparatively modern invention (late nineteenth century). As many as forty different flavoring ingredients may be used in making a vermouth, which is why there is so much difference between one firm's product and another's.

In Europe vermouth is more often served by itself, as an aperitif, than in mixed drinks, and such a trend is growing in the United States. Other aperitif wines generically classed as vermouths include Dubonnet, Campari, and Byrrh.

Because of their brandy content, these fortified wines will remain drinkable almost indefinitely, even after being opened, as long as they are kept sealed or corked between times. However, it's advised that the drier fino sherries will retain their delicate flavor better if refrigerated after recorking.

Of Champagne, Voltaire is reputed to have written: "This fire where sparkling bubbles dance
Reflects the brilliant soul of France."

Vineyards in the Champagne district of France which includes 250 villages or plantations, covering an area of about 74,000 acres, located 90 miles northeast of Paris. Only three grape varieties are grown: the Pinot Noir and Pinot Meunier (black) and the Chardonnay, a white grape.

SPARKLING WINES

Certain wines, and no one knows why, undergo a second fermentation in the spring as they lie in their casks. This has always been so, and some of these wines retain their light natural sparkle, called "petulance," after being bottled. Among the best-known examples are the Vinho Verde wines of northern Portugal, Vouvray from the French Loire, and Lambrusco, the red, slightly sweet Italian wine. (Vouvray is sometimes a still wine, and sometimes deliberately turned into a sparkling wine by the champagne process. One is likely to find the "petulant" wine only in its local habitat. Nor do the Vinho Verde wines retain their petulance when shipped long distances.)

In the Middle Ages, when this second wine fermentation occurred in the spring, it often caused the stoppers in the wine casks to pop out, and the foaming wine would then run over the floor.

About 1700, the monk Dom Pérignon, cellar master in a Benedictine abbey in the Champagne district of France, tried making tighter stoppers with bark cut from the cork trees in the abbey garden, and fastened them to the bung holes with heavy cord. This was apparently the first time cork was used as a stopper—half a century at least before it was used in Portugal. The cork and the cord together did prevent the wine from bursting its "prison," but the fermentation inside the cask rumbled away unstopped. When these wines were uncorked the following year, according to legend, the monk is said to have rushed to his brother friars, crying out, "Come quickly, I've just been drinking stars!"

Today in making champagne-type sparkling wines, this second fermentation is not left to chance. After the raw wines have been ripened properly, then blended to achieve the desired degree of sweetness, they are racked and fined and given a dosage of sugar dissolved in wine and cultured wine yeasts. After this the wine is bottled and corked, and the corks are fastened with heavy wire, then the bottles are placed in cool storage rooms to await the second fermentation. Extraheavy glass must be used for the bottles and heavy-duty cork for the bung; even so, workers must wear masks in case of explosions in the storage rooms. In addition, bottles must be stacked upside down to prevent escape of the gas and storage temperatures must be kept very cool so fermentation will not proceed too rapidly.

Another method used to make sparkling wines is called the "bulk process": the wine is stored in huge, sealed tanks during fermentation, then transferred to bottles under pressure to retain the bubbles. When made this way, the label must carry the notation "bulk process."

Fine vintage champagnes are sometimes aged in bottle from four up to six years. This decision, like everything else in wine making, is made by the wine master, who alone is able to judge when and whether a wine is worthy of such an honor.

It used to be that most sparkling wines were white. Even the first "sparkling burgundies" produced by the champagne process in the Burgundy wine region of France were either white or a delicate pink. The first red sparkling burgundy was produced in the United States, and it is usually sweet. White champagnes range from brut, or very dry, to sec, literally French for "dry" but in reality faintly sweet, to demi-sec, and finally doux, or sweet.

Asti Spumante, most renowned of Italian sparkling wines, is always sweet, and so is a somewhat similar American sparkling wine called

Harvesting Champagne grapes takes about twelve days. Men, women and children cut the grapes, load them into wicker baskets which hold about 150 pounds, and these are immediately carried to the pressing rooms which are nearby.

Here, giant presses convert four tons of grapes into juice with great speed in three pressings, and the juice (or "must") flows into large oak or cement casks. Fermentation of this "must" takes place for several weeks, resulting in a still wine.

After bottling, the wine is stored on racks, lying flat, in deep underground cellars, where it matures for three to five years. *Note:* All operations connected with making French Champagne must, by law, take place within the limits of the vinebearing province of Champagne and in cellars into which no wine of other origin has been admitted.

After the first fermentation is thoroughly completed, the bottles are placed neck-down in racks shown here, and each bottle is turned about 45 degrees every day for approximately three months. A highly skilled operator can turn 30,000 bottles each day. This process ensures that the sediment in the wine will gradually sink down and accumulate in the necks of the bottles.

Moscato Spumante made from Muscat grapes. Cold duck (also sweet) is a cross between champagne and sparkling burgundy.

American champagnes made with native American grapes, those classed as *Vitis labrusca,* tend to have what is called a "foxy" flavor, but California vintners are increasingly using the European grapes Chardonnay and Pinot Noir to make champagnes more nearly like those of France. A number of other sparkling wines have recently been introduced, including Sparkling Gamay Beaujolais and Sparkling Vin Rosé.

"Crackling" is a term used to describe wines with less effervescence than those classified as "sparkling." In this country, such wines must be naturally fermented, as in the champagne process. (This is not necessarily true of imported crackling wines, however. Lancer's Crackling Rosé, for example, is a blend of still red and white wines artificially carbonated.)

In the last decade what are called "pop" wines, containing no more than 8 percent alcohol and made effervescent with added carbon dioxide, have proved especially popular with the younger generation reared on flavored sodas. Serious wine drinkers generally consider these an abomination, but we can hope that the young people being "weaned" on such drinks may graduate from them to a more critical appreciation of wine.

THE AMERICAN WINE REVOLUTION

Thomas Jefferson's plea from the White House that wine drinking be promoted as a matter of temperance and a civilizing influence was echoed by many of our Founding Fathers, and in the first decades of our history as an independent nation, there were predictions that the United States would become one of the leading wine-producing countries of the world.

Unfortunately, as we know, efforts to grow imported wine stocks from Europe, the *Vitis vinifera* varieties, met with failure. They were too delicate to survive in the East Coast climate. Native varieties were then planted and used with success. By 1850, the wine production in Ohio, Missouri, Pennsylvania, and Indiana had reached a scale that promised to bear out those hopeful early predictions, with Ohio's wine industry leading all others.

In California, by this same period, sons of Old World winemakers were proving that in their climate the European vines could thrive, and by the time California became a state, vineyards were already planted widely, and many who had rushed to the West to prospect for gold found greater fortunes were to be made with the "philosopher's gold" of wine.

But simultaneously with this progress in viticulture, a scourge that would devastate the American wine industry more effectively than phylloxera was the Temperance crusade. Its fanatic leaders lumped wine with other alcoholic beverages as "sinful," a tool of the Devil. First organized as early as 1803 in New York State, the influence of the Drys spread rapidly, until by the end of the century many states had already imposed local prohibition long before it became a federal law in 1920. Not only were wineries forced to close down, several generations of Americans were denied the opportunity of learning how much more gracious mealtime could be with a carafe of wine on the table.

Global travel during and after World War II sparked the gourmet trend that has changed all that. But in a nation where the choice had long been between highballs and cocktails for sophisticated adults and soda pop for nearly everyone else, dry wines at first had a hard time of it, since those not accustomed to wine drinking nearly always prefer sweet to dry wines at first (the more one drinks wine, the drier one's palate usually becomes). Indeed, in the first two decades after Repeal, sales of sweet dessert wines were three times that of table wines.

Then, in 1968, the tide turned. Now the opposite has happened: table wines lead dessert wines three to one. "Wine fever" has swept the country. Becoming a connoisseur is now fashionable. And this is the most important change of all, because no matter what advances the vintners themselves might make, wine making, like all arts, must have an appreciative audience to thrive commercially. It's a mark of our progress that the United States now has what is considered one of the finest schools of viticulture and enology in the world, at the University of California at Davis, attracting students from many Old World wine countries.

Further, in the brief forty-year period since Repeal, we, too, have begun producing great vintage wines. Some of the 1940 Cabernet Sauvignons of the Napa Valley, put away to bottle-age, have proved to have excellent bouquet after thirty years. And in just the last year, French wine experts participating in a blind tasting proclaimed that certain of the California Cabernets could be "brothers" to some of the "very greatest" Bordeaux wines. In particular, the French rated a 1969 Private Reserve Cabernet of Beaulieu Vineyards, selling for $6.30 a bottle, as in the same class with 1967 châteaux wines of the Médoc, some of which bring $30 a bottle (and upward) in American shops. The French experts also singled out for praise Louis Martini's Pinot Noir, Christian Brothers' Zinfandel and Gamay Noir, and Robert Mondavi's Mountain Pinot. As for Gallo's Hearty Burgundy, they found this to be a very good *vin ordinaire* for the price.

Technical progress has played a very important part in American viticulture. Sprinklers and wind machines are used to protect vines from frost, irrigation has been introduced in vineyards where rainfall is insufficient (the Salinas valley, once thought unsuitable for grapes, now gets all the water it needs pumped up from the Salinas River, discovered to be a great underground stream), and to reduce ravages from plant diseases, "heat treated vines" are being planted in new vineyards. Vines already virus free are selected, then raised in hothouses, where heat causes the vines to grow faster than the viruses, making virtually virus-free vineyards possible. This has resulted in both larger yield per acre and better-quality wine.

Both the Wente and Mirassou vineyards of California are now using mechanical grape harvesters to pick and crush the grapes, depositing them in tank trucks, where the wine-making process starts within five seconds after the grapes come from the vines. Already noted for the excellent quality of their wines, the Mirassou brothers assert that continual comparison tests have proved this method preserves flavor better and minimizes harmful oxidation. However, other vintners consider that hand picking is the sole way of selecting only the best clusters of grapes from the vines.

The process of experimentation goes in all directions. As some wine makers discard old, established methods for new techniques, others are restudying ancient and medieval texts, searching for still elusive

After the wine has aged for from three to five years, standing on end, neck down, the *dégorgement* takes place. This process removes all the sediment collected in the neck of the bottle by flash freezing. When the cork is pulled, the sediment is ejected in the ice, and the bottles are then recorked. Only then, according to French law, the bottle can—and *must*—carry on its label and on its cork "Champagne." In Europe, no sparkling wines can legally be called Champagne unless from this wine district and produced according to these long established methods. Such restrictions, however, do not apply to American sparkling wines called "champagne."

Baccarat Crystal—a graceful range of glasses designed for Champagne: left to right, the St. Remy Flute, the Dom Perignon Flute, the Laurent Perrier, the St. Remy #3 goblet, and the Short Tulip.

secrets of why certain wines turn out so much better than others.

Most wineries today store the casks in huge, vaultlike rooms above ground where climate is artificially controlled, but Robert Mondavi, after years of producing excellent wines in such storerooms, plans to try storing some of his wines underground and rolling the casks periodically, just to see what difference this might make.

With all the advances in techniques, the whims of nature still determine the final outcome of each vintage, and nothing else in wine making is more important than picking the grapes at exactly the right moment for each particular wine. The date of the harvest can only be guessed at in advance: tests of grape sugar must be made day after day as the time approaches, and the weather watched with prayers and supplication; then, when the grapes are ready, everyone in the winery must work around the clock in a feverish rush to get those precious grapes to the crusher at the magic moment.

Until the last few years, American vintners did much better with red wines than with white, with some of the Cabernets and Pinot Noirs in particular being labeled "great" by the most critical of wine drinkers, and with Zinfandel drawing ever more praise as a varietal. Zinfandel has a mysterious past: it is a *Vitis vinifera* variety, but no one is quite sure where it originated. It is not used as a wine grape in any other country. But the varietals by this name in California seem to get better with each year. It makes an excellent rosé, and there is even a pleasant white Zinfandel.

But now many outstanding white wines as well as red are coming from American wineries. Besides Pinot Chardonnay and Johannisberg Riesling, a delightful dry white wine made from Sauvignon Blanc grapes is variously called Dry Sauvignon, or Blanc Fumé, or Fumé Blanc. The

Sauvignon Blanc grapes, grown in the Livermore, Santa Clara and San Benito vineyards; widely used in the production of white wines.

Some of the Paul Masson Winery's oak and redwood aging casks at their champagne and wine cellars in Saratoga, California.

latter name was first given to it by Louis Martini, who had learned that this was the name given to the same grape variety when used in making Pouilly-Fumé (not to be confused with another French wine from another region, Pouilly-Fuissé, a luscious superb white from Burgundy) in France's Loire Valley—though the same grape in Bordeaux is called Sauvignon Blanc. Now Fumé Blanc is used by so many California wineries it has become a standard varietal name.

Several California wineries are now producing excellent Gewürztraminer, a semidry white wine with a distinctly spicy fragrance, made from a grape of Alsatian origin.° One of the best of all the American Gewürztraminers is being produced in Washington State, by the Ste. Michelle winery.

It's the smaller wineries that are producing the finest wines, which is nearly always the case. When mass production is introduced, something of that special attention a wine must have is usually lost, even when a skilled wine master is in charge.

Beautiful headquarters for Inglenook Vineyards of Napa Valley, California.

A change that may or may not augur well for the future is the way the big conglomerates are taking over some of the most renowned of the California wineries. Paul Masson and Christian Brothers are both owned by Seagram; Almadén, by National Distillers; Heublein-United

---

° Gewürztraminer is not the same varietal as Traminer, a grape used extensively in the Palatinate wine region of Germany to produce light fruity wines. This and the term Riesling can be very confusing: Gray Riesling is an altogether different grape family, and the wine called Sylvaner Riesling is made with two different grapes, neither of them a true Riesling. But then think of all the confusion over the term Beaujolais. The California wines called Gamay Beaujolais are made from a different grape than the Beaujolais of France, which is made from a variety called Gamay Noir.

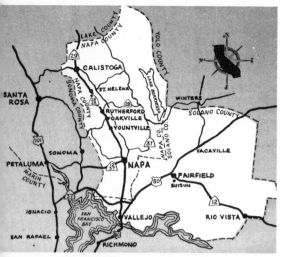

The Napa-Solano District is north of San Francisco, and abounds with wineries and vineyards, found on the valley floor and nestled in the surrounding foothills. Robert Louis Stevenson, inspired by the picturesque wineries and beautiful valley, wrote, in part: ". . . the stirring sunlight, and the growing vines, and the vats and bottles in the cavern, made a pleasant music for the mind."

The "Old Carriage House" for aging of fine wines in French oak barrels, at the Charles Krug Winery in Napa Valley.

Vintners owns Cresta Blanca, Inglenook, and also Beaulieu Vineyards (popularly known as BV).* Nestlé's has purchased Beringer Brothers. When Pillsbury recently purchased the renowned Souverain vineyards, it sent a ripple of uneasiness through the gourmet world. If the superb Souverain wines continue to be made with the same tender loving care and high but costly standards, the public will benefit because these excellent wines will be in much wider distribution. But all too often, when a private winery is absorbed into a conglomerate, excellence takes second place to corporate profits, and individual supervision is lost on the assembly line. We can at least take comfort in the trend as an indication of how seriously Big Business is viewing the future of America's wine industry.

Altogether there are more than five hundred commercial wineries in the United States, but 60 percent of the production is in the hands of a few giants, and only 5 percent of wine production is given to premium varietals. But there are so many smaller vintners making truly splendid wines, and more every year, that individual enterprise is far from squashed.

Typical of what is happening is the story of Sterling Vineyards, a family-owned enterprise whose Napa Valley vineyards were first planted as recently as 1964, and their first wines not produced until 1969. Michael Stone, vice-president and general manager, confessed that their only qualifications for starting a winery was a liking for wine, but they hired three Davis men as technicians, two to manage the vineyards and the third as wine master. Still only producing six different wines, these have proved to be so superior that in the spring of 1974, the winery's four proudest wines were introduced in ten major cities, though the owners are determined to remain small, using only grapes grown in their own vineyards, aged and bottled on the premises, and in California sold only at the winery, a striking white building on the crest of a hill that can be seen for miles. Besides three excellent white wines (Blanc de Sauvignon, Chenin Blanc, and Pinot Chardonnay), Sterling was the first to introduce a red wine called Merlot, one of the grapes used to produce the red wines of Bordeaux. Their 1969 Cabernet Sauvignon is a truly magnificent wine, though supplies of this, their first vintage wine to be introduced, are now all but exhausted.

Many California wineries, to encourage visitors, have constructed magnificent buildings with large tasting rooms, and they schedule regular tours through their plants, during which visitors are told about every step of wine making. Several of these wineries have picnic areas, and one, Château Souverain, has a first-class restaurant on the premises; others, like Robert Mondavi, present free cultural events, such as concerts, on the grounds, on the theory that wine is related to all the arts, an inseparable part of the finer things of life.

Wine people are a special breed. One finds a joyousness among everyone connected with the wine business; all seem to be truly enthusiastic about their work. Winery owners share a camaraderie with their

* The initials BV are frequently used to refer to Beaulieu Vineyards, but must not be confused with Buena Vista, one of the earliest commercial vineyards in California. Established in 1856 by the legendary "Count" Haraszthy, the vineyards had been long abandoned and the wine caves collapsed when in 1941 the estate was purchased by Frank Bartholomew. Now under still different management, Buena Vista wines are not in the same quality class as those of Beaulieu.

competitors, and there is a continual interchange of information among them. They drink one another's wines and also European wines in their homes, not just their own, and travel abroad frequently to taste and learn at other vineyards.

Not only do sons follow in their fathers' footsteps, but frequently so do grandsons and even, in some cases, great-grandsons. The Mirassou family has been in the wine business for five generations, with younger sons in training to carry on the tradition.

Longevity also seems to be characteristic: many an octogenarian is to be met on the premises of a winery or at wine festivals. Among them is Mrs. Isabel Simi Haigh, of the Simi Vineyards in Sonoma Valley, who began working in the family winery with her brothers when she was only fourteen. Today, at the age of eighty-three, last of the clan, she can be seen out front every day supervising the Simi tasting rooms.* The owner of the California Wine Association, producers of Eleven Cellars wines, is ninety-four-year-old Antonio Perelli-Minetti who has been a vineyard worker since he first came to California from his native Italy in 1902 and now runs his own winery, with the assistance of his three sons.

The Taylor Winery in New York State is still a family-run business, as it has been since 1880 when Walter Taylor, a master cooper, first began producing table wines, which he peddled himself in barrels on the streets of New York City. And while one member of the family, grandson Walter S. Taylor, is no longer part of the original enterprise, he has remained in the wine business, and his success with wines from hybrid varieties—not only the much-admired Baco Noir, but also a silky white Seyval Blanc and other wines that have brought critical praise—augurs well for the future.

Two other New York vintners are also making American wine history. Gold Seal Vineyards at Hammondsport in the Finger Lakes district now has the largest acreage planted in *Vitis vinifera* grapes of any Eastern winery. This is due to French-born and -trained Charles Fournier, winemaster at Gold Seal since 1934, who insisted there was no reason why the same grape varieties that thrived in the northernmost wine districts of France and along the Rhineland should not do equally well in New York climate. He planted the first Pinot Chardonnay and Riesling grapes in the East and proved his theory. Both the Gold Seal Blanc de Blancs champagne which bears the Charles Fournier signature and the still white wine called Chablis Nature are made with a blend of Pinot Chardonnay and French hybrid varieties, and the winery is also experimenting with production of a white wine made of 100 percent Pinot Chardonnay as well as a Johannisberg Riesling.

It was Charles Fournier who brought Dr. Konstantine Frank to this country, originally to work for Gold Seal. Dr. Frank, Russian born and trained in both French and Swiss wine schools, now has his own winery where he produces what many have called the finest of all

The Christian Brothers Novitiate and vineyards at Mont La Salle in the Napa Valley, at the crucial time of harvest.

---

* Simi Vineyards has another unique distinction: its wine master is a young woman, Mary Ann Graf, an Ohio girl who comes from a family of teetotalers. She had no interest in wines whatsoever until she became a student at the University of California at Davis, yet today she is the only female wine master in the business. Like all wine masters, hers is the final judgment at each step of wine making, and two of the Simi varietals, a Rosé Cabernet, and a Fumé Blanc are her "babies." The latter has a bouquet that is somehow suggestive of ripe figs, a fruity, almost heavy white wine.

American Johannisberg Rieslings. Dr. Frank sold his first Riesling at $45.00 a bottle and it outsold German wines costing $15.00. Today Dr. Frank's Johannisberg Riesling is considered a bargain, if it can be found, at $5.95. His Chardonnay and Pinot Noir, in smaller distribution, have received comparable praise.

Philip Wagner of the Boordy Vineyards predicts that there will be more sweeping changes in the American wine industry in the next twenty years than in the last twenty. It takes that long, he explains, first to develop strains that will thrive and produce fine wines in quite different climate zones, then for the long period of cask and bottle aging to achieve the essential ripeness, and finally, equally difficult, to gain public acceptance.

An aerial view of Gold Seal Vineyards, located in the heart of "The Champagne District of America," at Hammondsport in New York's Finger Lakes region. Gold Seal's Blanc de Blancs Champagne won the only gold medal awarded champagnes in the California State Fair of 1950. Other Gold Seal wines include Sparkling Burgundy, white and rosé table wines, appetizer and dessert wines.

VARIETAL WINE GRAPES

The better-established varietal names are being used increasingly in other countries. Many French wines are being so labeled; one Bordeaux red, for example, is called Cabernet Merlot, with no indication of the vineyard, and white wines from the Burgundy region are called Chardonnay. Almost every wine country is now producing a Cabernet and a Riesling, and the name Pinot Noir is increasingly being seen on imported wine labels. Thus, anyone who wishes to be knowledgeable about wine needs to understand what these varietal names mean. The following list may help.

Alexander: The first American wine produced commercially came from a native grape, named after John Alexander, gardener to William Penn, who discovered it growing wild on the banks of the Schuylkill

River. In pre-Prohibition days, one of the most popular of all wines with Americans, but now used primarily for blending by New York State and other Eastern wineries, for generic clarets and rosés. A *Vitis labrusca* grape classification.

Aurora: A French hybrid used in making a semidry white wine. Also known as Seyve-Villard. Considered to have great promise for the future. At present, best example is the Bully Hill varietal Aurora Blanc.

Barbera: A grape of Italian origin, where it is used to make a Piedmont wine of this name. Increasingly popular as a California varietal, it makes a full-bodied, robust wine, deep red in color.

Cabernet Rosé, or *Rosé de Cabernet:* A pink or rosé wine made from the Cabernet Sauvignon grape.

Cabernet Sauvignon: One of the five grape varieties used in making the renowned red wines of the Médoc (Bordeaux), and a leading varietal in California, though the California Cabernets tend to be softer and have their own distinct characteristics. All are astringent when young, aging to exquisite body. The vintage year, when given, is important as an indication of whether the wine has yet fully ripened; it should never be drunk young. Uncork well in advance of serving.

Carignane: A grape used primarily for blending in red wine production, though a few California wineries are now producing a varietal by this name. It must be drunk while very young, like a "nouveau" or harvest wine.

Catawba: A native American grape that makes a sweet white or pink wine, sometimes used in making New York State champagnes. Pink Catawba, Sparkling Catawba, and Catawba Vin Rosé are all to be seen in American wine shops, popular with those who like sweet wines and don't object to the characteristic "foxy" flavor of Catawba.

Chardonnay or *Pinot Chardonnay:* The principal grape variety used in making Chablis in the Burgundy wine region of France, and blended with Pinot Noir grapes for champagne. In California, considered the finest of all white wine varietals. Needs longer aging than other white wines, should be flinty dry.

Chenin Blanc: The grape used to make Vouvray in the Loire Valley and for a wide range of white wines in California, ranging from quite dry to semisweet. Christian Brothers produces both a semisweet Chenin Blanc and a dry white wine, made with the same grape, called Pineau de la Loire.

Concord: A native American blue-skinned grape used primarily for grape juice, jams, and jellies until it was discovered to be ideal for kosher-type wines. Syrupy sweet.

Delaware: Another *Vitis labrusca* or native grape, used in making New York State and Ohio champagnes and also for white wines that may bear the generic name "sauterne."

An old world art tradition carried on at the Sebastiani Vineyards aging cellars in Sonoma. Earle Brown is shown carving grapes on a large barrel with his own hand-made tools. Completion of such a design may take as long as a month, depending on its intricacy.

Ernest and Julio Gallo's labels.

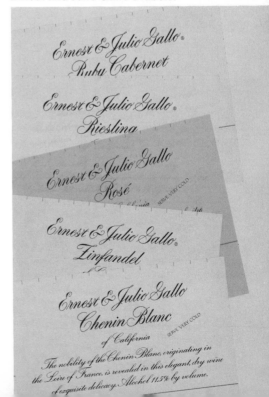

Eight Gallo wines displayed, showing the remarkable variety of grape types which have been transplanted from Europe and successfully grown in California. The French Colombard, a white wine grape, comes from the Cognac district in France. It is used largely in California for making Chablis and semisweet wine. The Cabernet is a superb red wine grape used in the Clarets of Bordeaux, and in the north coast counties of California for making America's best red wines. Chenin Blanc comes from the Provinces of Loire, Touraine and Anjou; and grows well in the northern California counties of Sonoma, Napa and Santa Clara. Riesling grapes, known also as White Riesling or Johannisberg Riesling, are used for making very good dry white wines. The Sauvignon Blanc is a native of Bordeaux, now thriving in Livermore and San Benito counties; the Barbera is grown in the coastal valleys of California, having been transplanted from the Piedmont region of northwest Italy. The wine is deep red and full-bodied and makes a good accompaniment for Italian food. The Zinfandel is the most widely planted red wine grape in California; it was grown there in pre-Civil War days.

Johannisberg Riesling grapes, from which a very good, dry, white wine is made in cooler regions of California.

Emerald Riesling: A hybrid developed at Davis in California, used by Paul Masson to make the dry white wine called Emerald Dry. Of no relation to the Johannisberg Riesling grape.

Foch: A French-American hybrid used for making a wine ruby red in color, considered to hold great promise.

French Colombard: A *Vitis vinifera* variety formerly used only for blending but now frequently the principal grape in a white varietal, semisweet to sweet, increasingly popular in California. Oakville's French Colombard 1972, a dessert wine, was highly praised. Many are semidry.

Fumé Blanc: See Sauvignon Blanc.

Gamay Beaujolais: A grape variety used in making a light red California wine, but not the same grape used in France to make the wine called Beaujolais (which is named after its area of demarcation). The latter is made with a grape called Gamay Noir. At least one varietal called Gamay Noir has also appeared in California. A wine called Gamay Rosé is made with the Gamay Beaujolais grape, and there is also a Sparkling Gamay Beaujolais.

Gewürztraminer: A spicy, full-bodied aromatic white wine from a grape of Alsatian origin. Its bouquet can be almost overpowering; and it ranges from semidry to semisweet. Several West Coast wineries now produce it as a varietal; so do wineries in Germany, Austria, and Switzerland.

Gray Riesling: An altogether different grape variety from Johannisberg Riesling, it produces a pale, light white wine, usually quite acidic.

Green Hungarian: The name is more intriguing than the wine, which is disappointingly light, with very little body; it ranges (according to the winery) from very dry to medium sweet. Formerly used only in blending.

Grenache: The grape used in making Tavel rosé, in the Côtes du Rhône, it is now one of the top favorites of all rosé varietals in the United States. Used only for making rosés until Almadén introduced a red wine, Grenoir, made with the same grape.

Johannisberg Riesling: The grape used in making the most renowned white wines of the Mosel and Rhine valleys, named after the Schloss Johannisberg vineyards, one of the most famous in the Rheingau wine district. Also sometimes called White Riesling, but not to be confused with Gray Riesling. Many less expensive wines called "riesling" are sometimes made with Sylvaner or other white wine grapes.

Muscat Canelli or *Muscat de Frontignan:* A grape with great natural sweetness used for dessert wines and for blending. The grape is also popular for eating.

Pedro Ximénes: Another naturally sweet wine grape of Spanish origin, one with a very old history. Used in making the sweeter Spanish sherries. A wine by this name was popular in colonial America; Jefferson ordered it by the pipe.

Petite-Sirah: Used in the Rhône valley (Provence) to make the heavy, robust, velvety red wines of which Châteauneuf-du-Pape is the best known. Varietals of this name (and made with the same grape) in California also become deep red and robust with aging, but when young tend to be light and very tart. Petit Rosé, the driest of the rosé wines, is also made with this grape.

Pinot Blanc or *White Pinot:* Another name for the Chenin Blanc grape, not related at all to Pinot Chardonnay.

Pinot Chardonnay: See Chardonnay.

Pinot Noir: The grape used to make the fabulous red wines of Burgundy and also for one of the most admired of California red varietals. Needs long aging and uncorking an hour or so before serving.

Pinot St. George: Of the *Vitis vinifera* family, the origin of the grape is as much a mystery as that of Zinfandel. Christian Brothers makes the only varietal carrying this name, a tart, light red wine, one of their most popular wines.

Riesling: See Johannisberg Riesling.

Ruby Cabernet: Used primarily for blending, this is a hybrid developed at Davis, though recently Gallo introduced a varietal wine with the name. Dark red in color, with fruity flavor, it should improve with age.

Sauvignon Blanc: One of the grapes used in making the sweet white wines of the Sauternes district of Bordeaux, and under a different name, Fumé Blanc, for making Pouilly-Fumé in the Loire. In California, many distinctly different wines are made with the grape—some dry, some sweet, some semisweet. Dry Sauvignon Blanc as produced at Sterling Vineyards is much the same as the wine called Fumé Blanc by some vintners, Blanc Fumé by others. The Oakville Sauvignon Fleur is a flowery sweet dessert wine.

Scuppernong: Not a true wine grape but a "cluster grape," from which a very sweet, rich white wine is made, primarily in North Carolina.

Seibel: See Aurora. A considerable number of French-American hybrid grapes have this name followed by a number, such as Seibel 5279 or Seibel 7053, but these designations are used only in the nursery.

Sémillon: Also used in making the Sauternes of France, the varietals carrying this name in California are mostly semisweet to sweet, but there are also a few dry Sémillons.

Seyval or *Seyve-Villard:* A French hybrid which makes a crisp, dry white wine. The Bully Hill Seyval Blanc is an excellent example. *See also* Aurora.

Petite Sirah grapes, widely planted in Napa and Sonoma counties, are used mainly in the production of California Burgundy, though also increasingly as a varietal with this name.

Inglenook Vineyards' cask bottling of 1970 Pinot Noir and Red Pinot took place in 1974. The wine had been aged in 200-300-gallon oak casks at the Winery in Rutherford.

Inglenook's Navalle Chenin Blanc and Navalle Zinfandel shown here in Magnum Decanters and ordinary size bottles.

These vineyards, located in the coastal sections of California's steep hills, must be cultivated by horses. Sleds are used to bring the ripe grapes down to the wineries during harvest season.

Sylvaner: Of German origin, the grape makes a light, fruity white wine, semidry. Sometimes called Sylvaner Riesling or Franken Riesling, many of the wines called "riesling" are really made with this grape. Should always be well chilled before serving.

Traminer: Similar to Sylvaner, some wine experts have called this the same varietal as Gewürztraminer, but a shortened name. Others insist it is an entirely different grape variety. In any case, it, too, makes a pleasant dry to semidry white wine.

Zinfandel: Of undetermined origin, this *Vitis vinifera* grape has come into its own in California, where the varietals bearing the name are among the most popular of all the reds. Less costly than a Pinot Noir or even a Barbera, and maturing fairly early for a red, they have intriguing zest, good tannin, and a bouquet that has been variously described as "brambly," reminiscent of raspberries, or with something of the same scent as geraniums. Even as a jug wine, it is pleasant. Zinfandel Rosé is deeper in color than other pink wines, drier than most, and almost like a light red wine.

PROPRIETARY NAMES

Increasingly, American vintners are bestowing their own brand names on certain of their wines, blends of more than one grape variety—sometimes of three or four—wines they consider sufficiently unique and of superior quality to so honor. Some examples: Paul Masson's Rubion and Baroque wines, both red, and Emerald Dry and Rhine Castle, both white. Christian Brothers has given its own name to Château La Salle, a sweet white wine, and Pineau de la Loire (a dry Chenin Blanc) is proprietary.

Almadén recently introduced its light red Grenoir Original; Inglenook has its Charbono, a red; Beringer Bärenblut is also a red, a blend of Pinot Noir and Grignolino grapes. Boordy Blümchen is the proprietary name of a white wine of the Boordy Vineyards in New York State. Gallo Hearty Burgundy can also be considered a proprietary name. Wine Growers Guild had such success with its slightly sweet red table wine called Vino de Tavola that it now has a white wine bearing the same proprietary name.

The custom is not new. The German wines Blue Nun, Liebfraumilch, Moselblümchen, and Zeller Schwarze Katz are all commercial names for wines from many different minor vineyards or cooperatives, blended to produce standardized products.

The Portuguese rosé wines, all of which were developed especially for overseas trade, carry proprietary names, and the Hungarian wine Egri Bikavér, which means "bull's blood," is also a standardized blended wine, some of which tastes suspiciously as if it might have been adulterated.

Many vintners use descriptive names for wines that are somewhat better than *vins ordinaires,* but not good enough to carry varietal labels. The term "mountain wine," for example, is frequently used. Once this indicated a superior wine, since the best wines are grown on mountain slopes, but now it is simply a trade term and all the wines are blends, some of which may have come from valleys, or from several regions.

Inglenook has an entire line of wines which bear the name Navalle. Taylor calls certain of its wines "lake country." But all these are commercial terms, meant to make the wine seem special, when usually it means simply that they are not fine enough for varietal names or vintage labeling. The wineries do, on the other hand, attempt to keep these products standard, year after year, through blending. Such phrases as "reserve," "cask," and "special selection" are also commercial appendages without established designation in this country.

NAMES TO REMEMBER, NAMES TO IGNORE

An unusually impressive wine cellar, found at Château La Mission-Haut-Brion in the Graves district of Bordeaux. To the right is a locked and barred area holding special reserves of this superb Claret.

Generic classifications were originally introduced to make wine selections more simple for Americans, but they are so often misleading, it would be my advice for the beginning wine drinker to disregard both generic and varietal names and select wines on the basis of being red, white, or rosé. Only with time and with considerable critical drinking does one learn which wine makers turn out the finest wine in each class or type, and price is not always a reliable criterion.

As an example of how confusing even generic names can be: "claret" supposedly means a lighter-bodied, crisper wine; "burgundy," one more full-bodied and velvety. When the English gave the name "claret" to the red wines of Bordeaux, it was before the time of bottle aging, and then the young wines well deserved the name. But a vintage Bordeaux is no longer a light wine, it has developed assertiveness and deeper

Four representative French wines: Châteauneuf-du-Pape comes from the Rhône Valley in southern France; the Fleurie is an excellent Beaujolais from the town of the same name; Château Haut-Brion is considered one of Bordeaux's greatest red wines; and the Pouilly-Fuissé, a Burgundy, is a wonderful, dry white wine.

The oldest wine cellar in Bordeaux (and probably in all of France) was carved out of a single monolithic rock by the Romans. It is part of Château Ausone which produces a very fine St. Emilion.

color and body because of the tannin. On the other hand Beaujolais, from the Burgundy region (the southernmost part of Burgundy), is a light red wine that, because it must be drunk young, never becomes robust. If aged in bottle, instead of developing depth, Beaujolais only goes flat; it never acquires that velvety quality possessed by Burgundy reds from other areas of the wine region to the north.

The same confusion marks American red wines called "clarets" or "burgundies." Whether a claret is indeed light and a burgundy heavier depends on the individual winery. Industry-wide standards even for blended wines are not yet established.

As for the generic names used for white wines, "sauterne" (no final s) in this country means a dry white wine, whereas in France, Sauternes (spelled with a final s) means a semisweet to sweet wine usually recommended to be served with dessert. Actually, because the American public still demands table wines to be somewhat on the sweet side, certain of the American wines called "sauterne" turn out to be almost as sweet as the French Sauternes, but they are served nevertheless as "dry" wines with meals.

"Rhine wine" is supposed to be still drier than "sauterne," but some carrying this label, especially among the jug wines, are anything but dry. The same criticism can be made of American wines called "chablis"; and "pink chablis" is a ridiculous paradox of a name—logically there could be no such wine!

But varietal names also can be misleading. For example, Chenin Blanc is the name of the grape used in France to make Vouvray, a semisweet white wine. But in California now some wines called Dry Chenin Blanc are proving to be as dry as a Moselle (or Mosel), and Wente Brothers' Le Blanc de Blanc, made from a blend of Chenin Blanc and Ugni Blanc grapes, is a beautifully dry, fragrant white wine. And the wine called Chenin Blanc of Sterling Vineyards, a blend of Pinot Chardonnay and Chenin Blanc grapes, is a full-bodied, almost heavy dry white wine, with a smoky aftertaste and a heady bouquet that altogether defies description.

Then consider Green Hungarian, grapes that were originally used only in blending. When Frank Bartholomew, a San Francisco newspaperman, purchased the old Buena Vista vineyards, he became intrigued by the name Green Hungarian and introduced a wine made from the grapes as a new varietal, a semisweet white wine. Now many of the wines called Green Hungarian are decidedly tart. And so it goes. Even Pinot Chardonnay, considered by many the finest varietal white of California, differs enormously from one vineyard to another, as does Johannisberg Riesling.

It has become as important to observe the name of the vintner as the generic and varietal names when selecting wines, and to learn that an enormous amount of tasting and testing may be required to discover one's favorites. Wine preferences are so highly personal that a wine that causes one gourmet to wax extravagant with praise may not be liked at all by another, equally enthusiastic wine lover.

Many wineries now add bits of description to their labels, telling the buyer, for example, that this is a semidry, or "moderately dry" white wine, or that a red wine is "mellow." But when this latter term is used on the label of bulk-produced American wines, it often turns out to mean that the wine is more sweet than a table wine should rightly be.

"Dry" is the most misleading of all wine terms. It means "lacking in sweetness," but that can cover the waterfront. How much sweetness is lacking is the question. Yet a wine that may seem to my tastes delightfully dry, to another person could seem sour.

I have never forgotten what happened with a bottle of French Cordon Bleu brut champagne that was delivered to me as a bon voyage gift when I was sailing once for Europe by freighter. I gave the bottle to the steward to be chilled, but as it happened, a proper occasion for opening the champagne did not occur until some days later. When finally I requested that I would like the champagne to be served in my cabin, a look of horror spread over the steward's face. By mistake, he had served it the very first night to a young couple, thinking it was theirs. And when I asked them about this, I was the one to be even more horrified. They confessed they hadn't really liked it. For them, this costly vintage champagne was much too dry!

FRENCH WINES

With prices of the famous Burgundy and Bordeaux wines now astronomical, French wine exporters are currently sending many so-called country wines (*vin du pays*) and *petits châteaux* wines to the United States. Some of these are very good indeed. One that seems invariably to hold up well is an inexpensive red wine from southern France, near the Bordeaux wine region but in an unclassified district, Coteaux de Tricastin. Others that do carry the Appellation d'Origine Contrôlée, meaning that they are verified as having been produced in a specified wine region and measuring up to certain established standards, turn out sometimes to be disappointing. They may be from recognized wine districts, yet be minor wines. In other cases, so little information about the regions of origin is given on the label that the average wine buyer can only take them on faith, and he may or may not be rewarded.

Probably just a very small part of Château Climens' superb production of Barsac, a Sauternes, and a truly great dessert wine.

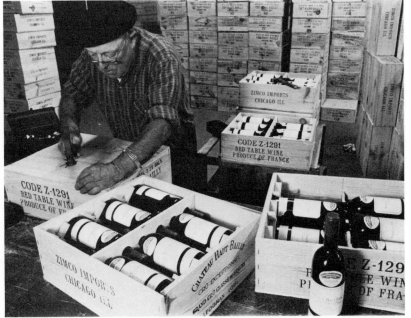

Next stop Chicago! for this shipment of Château Haut-Bailly, a Claret from the Graves district of Bordeaux.

Beaujolais, produced in the southernmost part of the Burgundy wine region, has always been a "young wine," meaning it should not be expected to develop great body and character, yet somehow it seems these days much thinner and lighter than it used to be.

Besides the great Bordeaux châteaux wines mentioned earlier, place names of origin to look for on labels of red wines from Bordeaux include Saint-Julien, Saint-Émilion, and Pomerol. With age all of these develop immense bouquet and a tingling assertive aftertaste. They should not be drunk when young.

From the Graves region come both red and white wines; the whites are crisp, a little acidic. The white wines of the Sauternes region are always on the sweet side, but with wonderful fragrance.

While the great names of Burgundy (Nuits-Saint-Georges, Le Corton, Mâcon, Clos de Vougeot, Pommard, Romanée-Conti) are now fantastically expensive, wines from the Burgundy region bearing varietal names, Chardonnay or Pinot Noir, are special enough to serve with pride.

From the Loire Valley, Muscadet is a pleasant, fruity white wine, to be drunk young. Vouvray has already been mentioned. Several rosé wines also come from the Loire.

A number of wines from Provence are now appearing with quite reasonable price tags. Corbière, a fairly light red wine from France's Mediterranean coast, is in the same class as the Italian Bardolino. The most renowned of red wines from southern France is Châteauneuf-du-Pape, very heavy, very smooth. Another, labeled simply Côtes du Rhône, is sometimes heavy and quite high in alcohol for a table wine, but again may be light and fresh. For the price (around $2) it is generally an excellent buy.

French wines always bear the date of vintage on the label. Keep in mind that this should be weighed against the keeping qualities in the wine. For a wine that does not age well, observe the vintage year as a guide to whether it will still be good. If it's a red Bordeaux or Burgundy that needs age to mature, keep it, if you can, until it is at least five years old. If it's Beaujolais, drink it right now.

© 1969, Walter S. Taylor, Greyton H. Taylor Wine Museum

The Chelois grape, now a French-American varietal, was developed in France in the late 1800s; it was brought to this country after World War II. It is considered one of the most outstanding varietals grown in the Finger Lakes District of New York State.

GERMAN WINES

A German wine label tells you everything you need to know—the vintage year, the wine region, the town or village, perhaps the particular vineyard, and the grape variety. Equally important is the quality classification. *Qualitätswein* must come exclusively from one of eleven regions and is made from approved grape varieties. The highest categories are *Qualitätswein Mit Prädikat*; they are specially graded quality wines and must come from approved grape varieties. *Kabinett* are the lightest—usually dry, elegant and delicate; *Spätlese* (meaning late harvest) have more body and a degree of sweetness. *Auslese* are noble wines made from extra ripe, perfect grapes, pressed separately.

The eleven major wine-producing areas border the Rhine and its tributaries. The most famous is probably the Rheingau, producing world-famous Riesling wines which are full-bodied, with a rich bouquet. Among the famed Rheingau townships and vineyards are Schloss Johannisberg (schloss is the German equivalent of the French château), Schloss Vollrads, Hochheim, Rudesheim, Winkel and Bischofsberg.

Many people consider wines of the Mosel (Moselle in France) region

Example of the information a German wine label must contain as decreed in 1971 when a law was passed, defining the specific details which must appear.

RHEINHESSEN

1971er
WINZERDORFER
REBBERG
RIESLING

Weinkellerei XYZ

A.P. Nr. 438482281073
QUALITATSWEIN

more elegant than those from the Rheingau. The wines tend to be drier, and lighter, but with an equally persuasive—if more delicate—bouquet.

Liebfraumilch (meaning Blessed Mother's Milk) is the name of a type of wine and geographical designation, which has become the best-selling German wine in this country. Some are excellent, some decidedly inferior, so buy only those which carry the town of origin, or shipper's name, or a quality designation. Zeller Schwarze Katz (Black Cat), a wine from the Lower Mosel, is another popular name which can be equally misleading. Still another wine in the same category of indefinite origin, Moselblümchen (Little Flower of the Moselle) also tends to be overrated.

By and large, the best German wines are white. Those in the low- to medium-priced category should be drunk while fairly young—up to three years. However, the "big" wines of great vintage years, from famous towns or vineyards and with a quality control designation, have no such limitations. Those such as Spätlese or Auslese retain their vitality for decades, maturing to their peak in the bottle. They are considered to be remarkable wines, worth the high prices they command.

A representative display of German wines behind a map showing the eleven wine-producing districts and the rivers which they border.

Typical German vineyards climbing the steep banks of the River Rhine in the Mittelheim district.

Labels which represent some of Italy's finest wine exports, among which Chianti is probably the best known in the United States.

ITALIAN WINES

Though Italy is the world's greatest wine producer, the Italians consume most of what they grow themselves. Chianti, of course, is the name best known to Americans because of its availability in nearly all American restaurants and liquor stores—and its use as a generic name by American wine producers. "Classico" on an Italian label means it is one of the better wines of the producer, but whether or not it is in fact a superior wine depends on the vintner. Some chiantis are extremely harsh.

Very popular now and moderately priced are Soave, a superb white wine, and the dry red Valpolicella and Bardolino, all three from the Piedmont region. Other red wines from the same wine region, but commanding more respect from connoisseurs, are those called Barolo, Gattinara, and Carema. These are quite robust and should not be drunk young. If well aged, they can be velvety, with great "nose."

OTHER IMPORTED WINES TO LOOK FOR

Wines from Spain, Hungary, Portugal, Yugoslavia, Greece, Chile, even Australia are now being seen on shelves of American liquor stores.

The best of the Spanish table wines are the Riojas, both red and white. One of the finest of the Spanish reds available here is Marqués de Riscal; when well-aged, this can be comparable to a good French Burgundy. Others are very inexpensive, can be picked up on sale for under $1.50 a fifth or $4.00 for a demijohn (gallon). One of the finest for the price is Age (pronounced *ah-hay*), the red, white, and rosé all being well above average in quality for wines costing under $2.00.

From Portugal, red and white as well as rosé table wines are now being exported, the white sometimes called *vinho branco,* which translates literally as "white wine." The best of the red Portuguese table wines come from the Dāu district. These are comparable to French Burgundies, full and rich, aging to great mellowness. (Even better are the red and white Colares wines, but the Colares wine district is so small that none are exported.) Unique are the Vinho Verde wines from the north of Portugal. The name means "green wine," but this refers to age rather than color—they must be drunk young. All are dry and light in alcohol, and in their homeland have a natural petulance, but with shipping abroad, this is often lost. Found mostly in New York and Florida.

Chilean white wines are very good and very reasonable, especially the Riesling.

A few white table wines from Greece are available, the Domestika in widest distribution. Retsina, the resin-flavored white wine, is attractive to those who have spent some time in Greece, but it's an acquired taste, and most Americans are horrified by it.

Hungarian wines can be pleasant, especially the reds, but the greatest Hungarian wine is Tokaj, a collector's item, not the least like the American wine called Tokay. It's a natural wine, never fortified, varying from what is called "dry" to quite sweet, but even the dry is not meant to be served with meals.

Many Yugoslav and Chilean wines also now carry varietal names as well as generic, but each should first be tried on its merit. Quality is uneven; the Yugoslav Cabernet can sometimes be very good, with tremendous body and slightly astringent quality, but needs to be uncorked long before serving. Sipon is a nicely balanced dry white wine. Many wine drinkers consider the Yugoslav and the Spanish table wines to be currently the best bargains among the inexpensive imports.

A FEW TIPS ON BUYING AND STORING WINES

Start small: While still experimenting, buy half bottles whenever possible, and more than one of the same general classification for comparative testing. Only after you have found wines that particularly please you, *then* consider buying them in larger sizes, even perhaps by the case.

Always study labels: Even those labels which tell you very little are worth examination, since lack of specifics can be as telling as detailed classification. And remember, the more detailed the label information, the more superior the vintner himself considered the wine—though you may or may not agree with him. Wine classifications are still voluntary in the United States, but by taking note of such descriptive titles as "mountain" or "lake" wines, and terms like "estate bottled," you begin yourself to learn from experience how important (or sometimes unimportant) these terms can be.

The question of price: Many factors affect the price of a bottle of wine. The quality of the wine, of course, is of prime consideration, but there is also the question of how much individual attention it received at each stage of production, how long it was aged in cask and bottle, its availability or supply, local demand, and the cost of labor in the country where produced.

The *premiers crus* of French vintage wines, for example, cost far more because only a small proportion of the wine harvest, even in the most renowned vineyards, is set aside as deserving this mark of excellence. And any premium wine that has been aged in the bottle by the vintner for several years will cost more because of the storage space it must occupy—a reason for the consumer to buy up wines that promise to improve with age and to lay them away in his own "wine cellar," if he has one.

The very same wine of the same vintage year can be found for sale, at greatly differing prices, in different shops in the same city. This is as true of American wines as the imported ones. Prices in different cities, and in different parts of the country, vary even more. Gallo Hearty Burgundy, for example, may be found selling anywhere from $1.25 for a twenty-four-ounce bottle up to $1.70 for the same size. This is a good reason in itself to know your wines and check and compare prices. Then you can be sure when you are, or are not, picking up a real bargain.

Because a wine sells for a high price does not necessarily mean it is superior. Sometimes naïve customers will pay more because they see from a wine label that the wine is seven or eight years old, or older—not realizing that the wine may be so old it's not worth much of anything.

On the other hand, when you have learned to distinguish the difference, you will be the more ready to pay a higher price for wines that are truly excellent.

Never hesitate to serve a jug wine to guests if you judge it to be

Example of a wine label designating "1st Growth." Château Coutet is a great vineyard in the township of Barsac, Sauternes.

Grenache grapes, widely used in the production of Grenache Rosé in California. They are also used for a superior Port made in California, and for a new Almadén light red wine called Grenoir.

a really good wine for the price. It can always be served from a carafe if you bought it in a gallon container.

Try to avoid being a wine snob. It isn't always easy. When your palate has become critical, you may have to hold yourself in check to avoid speaking disparagingly about certain wines, and if you do express yourself too candidly before others whose tastes are not so educated, you will not endear yourself to them.

At the same time, avoid buying wines because they are "in," or even because you feel you must show off by paying a high price or displaying a label.

There is no one country which can claim exclusive superiority in wine production, including France. Every wine country has its excellent and its poor wines, and the bulk of the production is mostly in between these extremes. We can be proud that the American wine industry has made such superlative strides, and the more we "buy American," but critically, the better our wines will become.

(On the other hand, it's stupid to assert that we produce better *vins ordinaires* for the price than any other country in the world. That just isn't true. Maybe someday we will, when public taste has become more demanding, but anyone who has lived in a European wine country knows what really fine local wines are available at much less than the price we pay for pasteurized jug wines.)

Vintage wines: Only the most dedicated connoisseur, for whom wine study is a year-in, year-out obsession, can keep up with which were the best and which the poorer vintage years in the many wine countries of the world. More important is to learn which wines age well and which should be drunk young. Vintage charts cover only the most famous wine regions and quickly go out of date. However, even in California some vintage years have turned out far better than others, and as you get deeper into wine lore, you will begin to pick up vintage guidelines gradually.

Make friends with the wine merchant: Time was when the sales clerks in liquor stores knew so little about wines it was a waste of time to ask for their suggestions. Today all that has changed—especially if you patronize a store that specializes in wines and carries a big selection. If you start talking with a wine salesman about wine, let him know you are genuinely interested in knowing more and already have developed a palate; you will probably discover he is as enthusiastic about wine as you are. This is especially true of the younger salespeople. Keep coming back and asking their advice about good buys, and they may tip you off when special consignments come in.

How much to buy: For a tasting, it is usually recommended that you allow one-half bottle per person, that is, one-half of a twenty-four-ounce bottle, or twelve ounces. Some young people who have given wine tastings of their own tell me this is too much, since one is only supposed to take small sips of each wine. On the other hand, if it's a big wine and cheese party, that amount may be too little. It all depends on the thirst of the guests.

When wine is served at dinner, following before-dinner cocktails or aperitif wines, generally about one-third bottle per person will do, or one bottle to serve each three persons (two bottles for six). But if the wines are especially fine, you may find three bottles will be emptied before your delighted guests are ready to leave the table.

This Johannisberg Riesling Spätlese was made by Beaulieu Vineyard from grapes which had been left on the vines until they reached an almost raisin-like state. The climatic conditions in Napa Valley in 1972 were almost perfect for the Johannisberg grape.

For big wine and cheese parties (rather than tastings), purchase wine in half gallons, gallon jugs, or magnums (54 ounces) or demi-johns, a jug size roughly equivalent to a gallon. A wide selection of wines is now available in these larger bottle sizes, including "mountain wines" and generics from such premium wineries as Robert Mondavi, Wente, Louis Martini, and Weibel. Many of the more popular imported wines are now available in these larger sizes: Beaujolais, imported Chianti, Mateus Rosé, Age Rioja, and table wines from the Barcelona region of Spain. Besides, of course, the originators of jug wines: Gallo, Wine Makers Guild, Petri, and Cresta Blanca.

These three California Burgundies make an excellent choice for a small wine tasting party, served with crackers for clearing the palate between tastings.

Wine storage at home: The traditional reason for laying bottles on their sides is to keep the cork moist. Pasteurized wines with metal caps can just as well remain upright, as can the fortified wines.

If possible, keep wine in a room whose temperature is below 60 degrees Fahrenheit. Otherwise, store it in a place where the temperature is fairly even, away from any heat source. A closet under the stairs or in an interior room may do. Cellar storage is ideal—if dry and far from furnace heat or any pipes or ducts.

THE PROPER WAY TO SERVE WINE

When a bottle of vintage red wine is to be served, the cork needs to be removed at least an hour, preferably two hours, beforehand. This is referred to as letting the wine "breathe." And in a real sense, because wine is a living thing, after being cooped up so long in glass it needs to breathe in fresh, warm air to achieve the final stage in its magical transformation.

Once I was given two bottles of Château Haut-Brion as a hostess gift, and I excitedly uncorked one of them immediately to serve with lunch. What a disappointment! The wine was so harsh I could only think: Whatever caused Haut-Brion to have such a great reputation if this is typical? Or has the wine turned?

But the second bottle I saved for a special occasion, meantime reading up on Bordeaux wines and learning of the importance of uncorking in advance. Next time I opened the bottle three hours before dinner—and what a difference! When poured at table, we all agreed this was

The Sebastiani Vineyards in Sonoma, California, were established in 1825 on land first planted in wine grapes by the Franciscan Fathers of San Francisco Colano de Sonoma Mission. Samuele Sebastiani purchased the winery in 1904 and started making wine with Zinfandel grapes, a small press and a 501-gallon redwood tank. This family-owned winery now produces varietal reds, generic chianti, burgundy and Zinfandel, Rosés, varietal whites, and two sherries and a port.

a truly great wine. I would never have believed it was the same as the wine I tasted on that first occasion.

This miraculous change occurred for two reasons. For one thing, a fine wine should always be allowed to rest after the jogging and rough movement of being transported from place to place. Then it must be opened and given plenty of time to breathe so that the harshness of the tannin in the wine, brought into contact with air, mellows into softer texture and releases the complexities of bouquet and taste that make a wine great.

Why during its period of bottle aging must a wine be so carefully protected from oxygen, then when opened suddenly need a big whiff of oxygen to achieve subtlety and charm? I've listened to various explanations, and have carefully taken notes, but the suspicion lingers that no one really knows all the answers—yet. One change occurs during fermentation, another change while the wine rests in the cask, still another after it has been bottled, yet a fourth change when the cork is drawn. And while breathing is so important for aged wines, if they should get too much oxygen—that is, if they stand exposed to the air too long—the bouquet dissipates and the wine goes flat and sour.

What a temperamental creature this is that demands so much care, seems to take delight in dumbfounding the experts, yet when treated respectfully can completely enchant its admirers!

Vintage white wines quite as much as the reds need a rest after being purchased, and some of them benefit, too, by being uncorked in advance. This is a lesson to keep in mind when you purchase vintage wines for either a tasting or a dinner party. Be sure to buy supplies at least two or three days beforehand and lay the bottles on their sides in a wine rack (or keep them in the carton, as long as they lie horizontally) in a dark, reasonably cool place.

However, young wines and those of lesser quality will not necessarily benefit by being uncorked beforehand, and the pasteurized wines need not be opened at all until time to pour. The older a wine, the more gently it must be treated—but in return for such care, the rewards are great, at least for those with appreciative palates.

If a vintage white wine will improve with "breathing," how can one chill it after uncorking? The traditional way is to place it in a champagne or other similarly shaped bucket, surround the bottle with crushed or broken ice, and cover it all with a cloth napkin. Let the bottle stand in the ice for at least twenty minutes, turning gently once or twice. Or, the bottle can be uncorked for breathing, then the cork reinserted and the wine laid on its side on a refrigerator shelf to chill.

Actually, the bouquet of a fine white wine can be better appreciated if the wine is not chilled at all. This is something to remember if you are offering very special wines to friends or guests with critical palates. Further, many people make the mistake of chilling white wines too long, which robs them of their delicate flavor and may kill the bouquet. A very special wine, like a Spätlese of a French Sauternes, should be chilled only briefly, preferably in a wine or champagne bucket.

(Some very old wines—that is, twenty-five or thirty or more years in bottle, on the contrary, should not be uncorked in advance at all because of their fragility. But they should be served in large deep goblets for an appreciation of their long bottled-up bouquet.)

What happens when you order a vintage wine in a restaurant and it is uncorked before your eyes? Unhappily, you will not know it at its best. Ideally, you should order ahead, instructing the sommelier to uncork the wine for you in advance. But that would mean also ordering the meal ahead, to have the right wine with the food selected. Perhaps a compromise would be to order the food and wine as soon as you are seated, and demand that the wine be uncorked immediately, but giving it a minimum of fifteen minutes for breathing before it is poured.

How old can a wine be and still be drinkable? Even today, some wines thirty, forty, and even fifty years old have proved to be superb. Certain California wines put away to age shortly after the repeal of Prohibition when uncorked thirty years later were exquisite. A few of the great Cabernets and Chardonnays of 1968 and 1969 undoubtedly even now are locked up in private "treasure chests," destined to remain there until the year 2000.

In 1973, in the town of Freiburg, Germany, a hundred-year-old building was torn down, and what should be found buried beneath a stone pillar but a chest containing three bottles of wine. Two were white wines bearing a vintage label of 1865, a year so superb it was considered the vintage of the century, and the third was a red wine of 1868, almost as remarkable a year. Experts gently opened the three centenarian wines to taste them—and found all three had superlative bouquet and, further, two of the three were still exquisite in taste as well. Only one of the two whites had begun to turn. And this after, respectively, 105 and 108 years!

Treatment of wine after opening: If the wine is not consumed in one sitting, recork the bottle as tightly as possible and lay it again on its side. Or if the cork was damaged in opening or the corkscrew penetrated all the way through (making a hole through which the wine may drip), it's best to put it in the refrigerator, whether it's a white or red wine.

If when you uncork the wine again, you find it has turned slightly, one way you may still make use of it is to turn it into a punch, like sangria, adding fruit juice and soda. Sometimes you can also mix red and white for a "rosé" that is an improvement over either of the wines alone.

Learn to judge each wine by its own merit: Individual tastes differ so greatly that what some expert has praised, you may not care for at all, and a simple little inexpensive wine may seem to you extremely pleasant. Besides, a wine that is outstanding one year may not be nearly as good in a later vintage. This is, in fact, the great fascination of wine—learning how unique each is, how each has its own virtues and character.

A SIMPLE WINE GLOSSARY

When Robert Louis Stevenson visited California in the late nineteenth century, he found a name for the native wines: "bottled poetry."

Both poets and nonpoets have struggled for centuries to find the proper adjectives for describing what individual wines are like, and the words that have gradually come to make up a wine maker's vocabulary are sometimes strange indeed.

When a wine is described as "chewy" or "silky," obviously neither term can be taken literally. The drinker, trying to find a correct

A Napa Valley Landmark to commemorate its oldest operating winery, founded in 1861 by Charles Krug.

A semisweet Sauvignon Blanc, served with fruits and an almond-crusted Camembert, make a tempting and satisfying dessert.

description, succumbs to a lack of adequate vocabulary. The following definitions may be of help.

Acid. Quite tart, sometimes on the verge of being plain sour.

Aroma. See Bouquet. Aroma is the fragrance of the fruit, bouquet is the complex fragrance of the wine which develops with aging.

Astringent. A bit acid, puckery, with a clean kind of sensation.

Assertive. A wine with sharply defined character.

Balanced. The right combination of acid, natural grape sugar, tannin, and alcohol, giving to the wine a beautiful fragrance and a pleasant, lingering aftertaste.

Big. So heavy it "lies on the tongue."

Bone dry. Much the same as "crisp"; means that all the grape sugar has been fermented out, yet the wine, while tart, is not overly acidic.

Widmer's famous *solera* on the roof-top, with fifteen thousand 50-gallon white oak barrels holding sherry stock for four years of aging. It will then be blended with previously aged sherry in the cellars at the 87-year-old winery.

Botrytis cinerea. Botanical name of fungus that sometimes appears on grapes left on the vines very late to attain extra sweetness. The appearance of the grayish mold or growth is exciting to wine men because wines made from such grapes develop extraordinary bouquet and inimitable flavor. The mold affects not the pulp, but the skin only, causing it to wrinkle and shrivel, so that the grape contains less moisture but more sweetness. The fungus is sometimes referred to as "noble rot" (in French, *pourriture noble*) because the grapes apear to be almost rotten when picked.

Bouquet. No one has ever properly explained how this term, usually applied to flower arrangements, came to be used to mean the heady fragrance that invades the nostrils when one breathes in the fumes arising from a goblet of properly aged wine. An equally foolish term is increasingly in use: "nose." Of course it's your nose, not the wine's, that is doing the breathing—but there you are.

Bramble. Used to describe the taste of California's Zinfandel wines, which some have declared have a flavor reminiscent of raspberries —or perhaps they mean raspberry brambles?

Clean. Clear and pure, no hint of the cork in the flavor.

Corky. Said of a wine whose purity has been ruined by the presence of pieces of broken cork.

Crisp. Very, very dry but without the slightest touch of acidity, and with an aftertaste not at all sweet.

Dry. Lacking in sweetness. Some wines are described as semidry, meaning that they have a trace of sweetness. The vast majority of wine drinkers prefer wines that are not too acidic. Frequently, on the other hand, wines labeled "dry" are in fact semisweet, especially so with cheaper wines.

Finesse. Subtle, elusive, defying definition, but beautiful.

Flinty. Even drier than "crisp," almost tingling. The taste of the wine makes one think of the flinty soil in which its vines flourish.

Flowery. Soft, with a hint of sweetness (or maybe more than a hint, maybe semisweet) and a perfume-y kind of bouquet (q.v.).

Foxy. The peculiar taste of wines made with native *Vitis labrusca* grapes.

Free-run. The first juice from the grapes, extracted with gentle pressure or centrifugal force, as differentiated from a second pressing of the lees and sediment to extract what is called "pressed wine."

Fruity. One should never be able to detect the flavor of grape in a good wine, but when this term is used, it means you can almost, not quite, find an indefinable "fruit" flavor, one that has nothing to do with grapes.

Full-bodied. Said of a wine that seems to cling to your tongue, this describes a "round" taste, and a lovely, very smooth aftertaste as well. Most often applied to red wines.

Heavy. Said of a wine whose texture is indeed heavier, more clinging than that of other wines, the color deep (rich gold or dark purplish red), a wine you can almost "wrap your tongue around."

Light. The opposite of heavy. Most often applied to young wines that haven't yet, and may never, develop decided character.

Luscious. A term most frequently used to describe a wine with soft fruity flavor and big bouquet. More often applied to white semisweet or sweet wines.

Mellow. In American terminology, this usually means somewhat sweet. Applied to European wines, it means full-bodied and fragrant.

Must. The juice from fresh-picked grapes before or as it begins to ferment.

Noble rot. See *Botrytis cinerea.*

Nose. See Bouquet.

Pale dry. Used chiefly to describe sherries that are indeed pale in color and comparatively lacking in sweetness. Unfortunately, the description is often misleading, since such sherries may turn out to be not dry at all. Similarly, what are labeled "extra dry" vermouths can prove to be actually semisweet. With both these aperitif wines, one must learn to select favorites by brand name.

Persuasive. Usually refers to the bouquet (q.v.), one of overpowering loveliness.

Puckery. See Astringent.

Pungent. Decided character, not to be tossed off lightly, usually a bit on the tart side, though full bodied.

A one-ton plastic-lined tub containing grapes recently harvested by machine at Widmer's Wine Cellars in the Finger Lakes District of New York. The grapes are being dumped into a hopper for de-stemming prior to crushing.

California vineyards are a great tourist attraction. Here, visitors are being shown typical acres of vines disappearing and reappearing on the far-distant slopes.

Robust. Much the same as pungent, but suggesting a very well rounded and perfectly balanced wine.

Silky. See Velvety.

Soft. Not the least tart or assertive, a pleasant if sometimes unobtrusive wine.

Spicy. Used mainly to describe white wines with a perfume-y bouquet (q.v.) and smooth semidry flavor. It takes imagination to detect a definitive spice fragrance or taste, and yet it's a fuller, richer essence than from light dry wines.

Syrupy. Ultrasweet, almost like a liqueur.

Tart. Dry in an assertive way.

Tears. When the wine glass containing a very sweet wine is tilted, then turned upright again, a syrupy trail can be seen on the glass. Sometimes called "legs."

Thin. Term used to describe a wine without much character, either very young or made from very ordinary wine grapes.

Velvety. Said of a wine that has a very smooth effect on the tongue, but more robust than a wine called "soft." "Silky" means much the same except—well, the difference in texture between silk and velvet.

Vintage. The wine resulting from the grape harvest, which may be of poor or outstanding quality (when it is described as a "great vintage"). Even when there is an abundance of grapes, the quality may be poor—and vice versa, depending on that year's climatic conditions.

Vintage wines. Those regarded as so superior they are put away to develop their full potential with aging; also, wines that promise to improve with aging.

Vintage year. The year in which the grapes were harvested and crushed; even young wines are not usually ready to drink until the following year.

Watery. Said of a wine that's pretty bad, so weak or thin it could have been watered.

Woody. Said of a wine in whose flavor you can detect a suggestion of the oak barrel in which the wine aged, especially if aged in American oak. Aging in wood (especially French or Yugoslav oak) gives the wine fuller, richer flavor, but it should be so complex a bouquet and taste one cannot identify it as being like wood.

There are other phrases and terms that are bandied about lightheartedly by those who become absorbed in wine lore, and sometimes it seems as if their vocabularies multiply at an extraordinary rate. However, us ordinary souls needn't carry a phrase book around. If you are faced with an inadequacy of words for describing a wine, just forget everything else and call it "beautiful."

Every year the town of Nauvoo, Illinois, stages a grape festival that is marked by a unique ritual, known as "The Wedding of Wine and Cheese." This custom, begun by the French settlers who established Nauvoo in 1857, takes place in the town's 120-year-old wine cellars. The "bride" places a bottle of wine on a wine barrel, and beside it the "groom" places a wheel of cheese, then the mayor encircles the two with a wine-barrel hoop, symbolizing a wedding ring. The ceremony has particular significance, because when the Nauvoo winery had to close down during Prohibition, the cellars where wine had been aged for so long proved to be ideal for the culture of blue cheese, now a chief Nauvoo industry.

Cheese and wine not only make perfect partners gastronomically, the two have many, many things in common. Consider these, for example:

LEARNING ABOUT CHEESE

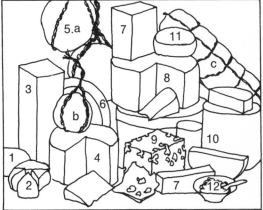

1. Smoky Gouda
2. Gouda
3. Muenster
4. Blue
5. Provolone
    a. Provoloni
    b. Provoloncinni
    c. Salame
6. Port du Salut
7. Brick
8. Cheddar
9. Swiss
10. Colby
11. Edam
12. Parmesan

1. All wine is made from grapes, nothing else. Yet there are hundreds of different wines, differing in color, taste, sweetness, body, aroma. All cheese is made solely from milk, yet the different cheeses of the world add up to well over a hundred varieties.

2. Both wine and cheese owe their transformation to enzymes or yeasts, which nature in her mysterious way plants in the original liquid—or, at least, this was true in the beginning. Today both the juice of wine grapes and the milk from which cheese is made are deliberately inoculated, but simply as a means of copying nature, not to leave it all to chance.

3. Cheese, like wine, must lie in deep cellars, caves, or cool storage rooms with controlled temperature while the enzymes create the fermentation that in cheese manufacture is called "curing."

4. Some cheeses must be consumed while young and fresh, others may be aged for as many as ten or twelve years, developing as they ripen quite different texture and flavor. This is comparable to the way in which some wines are at their best only when young, while others acquire magnificence with age.

5. Cheese nomenclature, like wine nomenclature, is confusing because of limitations. Many cheeses, like many wines, owe their names to the Old World town or region where they originated, though when copied in other countries the cheese may turn out to be altogether different. A Danish or an American Camembert, for example, may be as different from the original French cheese of the same name as a New York State Rhine wine from the dry white wines of Germany's Rhineland, or a California pale dry sherry from the original saline-piquant finos of Spain.

6. Both cheese and wine have ancient histories, and both from time immemorial have so delighted gourmets that they have been the subject of poetic wonder and extravagant praise.

CHEESE IN HISTORY

As many legends surround the origins of cheese as of wine. Probably the original cheese, like the first wine, "made itself" when curdled milk was strained and pressed into a cake. Certainly cheese has been produced deliberately for at least three thousand years, for cheese molds have been found in prehistoric ruins dating to that time or earlier. One of the earliest written references to cheese making is found in Homer's *Odyssey*, written about the eighth century B.C. When Ulysses, hero of the tale, and his men entered the cave of the one-eyed giant, Cyclops, they found pans of cheese in different stages of ripening on the shelves. (In another part of the same epic poem, a vineyard is described that is believed to be the prototype of the sherry vineyards of Spain, indicating that even then wine and cheese were already-established favorites.)

There are many cheeses still being made today much as they were in ancient times. England's Cheshire cheese, named after the town of Chester, was already in production when the Romans arrived in Britain. Of equally ancient origin is Cantal, the velvety-firm, tangy cheese of France, named after the regional *départemente* where it is produced. The cheese, traditionally molded in the shape of a drum, was singled out for praise by Pliny, the Roman naturalist, in his encyclopedic work of the first century. Roquefort's origin may be quite as old, or even older, for the cheese is made of the milk of sheep pastured in the mountains of southern France, in the same region where prehistoric cave drawings depict the ancestors of those same sheep, perhaps ten thousand years ago. The cheese's characteristic blue veining is caused by a spore absorbed from the walls of the high mountain cave where the cheese has for endless centuries been left to ripen.

HOW CHEESE IS MADE

All cheese is made from milk, but the first variance lies in the milk itself. In the United States today, all commercial cheese is made with cow's milk, but in other countries sheep's (ewes') and goat's milk cheeses are treasured, and some of these, imported here, are delighting new turophiles. Even when only cow's milk is used, there will be differences in the cheese according to the pasturage where the cows have grazed —not only the grasses and herbs on which they feed, but whether they pasture on high mountain slopes or in low valley pastureland, or whether the milk is gathered at night or in the morning.

The next step that helps mark the character of each cheese takes place when the curds, the milk solids, are separated from the whey, the liquid. To hasten this process, rennet is added and the cheese subjected to gentle warmth.

It is believed that the role of rennet was first observed by hunters or shepherds in the Old Stone Age when they put milk in goatskin flasks to carry with them for lunch, for rennet is a substance found in the stomach lining of all milk-bearing animals. It not only speeds the separation, but helps to keep the curds in a more homogenous mass rather than broken into small particles.

The amount of whey removed from the curds is a chief factor in determining whether the cheese will be soft, semisoft, semifirm, or firm. Soft cheeses, with much of the whey left in, are more perishable —because the bacteria that cause a cheese to spoil exist mostly in the whey rather than the curd. Yet it's among the soft cheeses that we find the most exotic flavors, those most likely to excite a gourmet's palate.

Fresh unripened cheeses are those made of the drained curd, eaten while fresh. What we call "pot" or "cottage" cheese is a prime example. Every milk-producing country of the world has such a cheese, known by different names. Cream cheese is also unripened, but it is made from milk much richer in fat content, the curd is cut in finer pieces, and lower temperatures are maintained during the separation of curd from whey.

To make ripened cheese, after the whey has been pressed out, the

Cheddaring at Dairylea—turning slabs of curd to remove whey. After this operation, the slabs are chopped into small pieces, salted and placed in 40-pound molds to be sent to aging rooms.

Taking a cylinder-shaped "core" of cheddar from a 40-pound wheel at the Dairylea cheddar plant in Adams, New York.

An aging room at the Dairylea cheddar plant; over four million pounds of cheddar are cured here for up to twelve months each year.

curd, packed in its molds, is left on shelves in the curing rooms, where the mysterious process of fermentation soon begins. Sometimes the gaseous bubbles breaking in the fermenting curd will develop into permanent holes. There may be many small holes, or a mixture of small and larger holes, or all may be enormous, as in Swiss cheese. Other cheeses, despite fermentation, may have no holes at all but remain solidly smooth.

In the olden days, cheese makers had no idea why such holes happened or did not happen. The "whys" are still something of a mystery, but modern technology has determined how to control the fermentation, both by the kind of culture with which the cheese is inoculated and by the temperature maintained in the curing rooms. When the curing rooms are warmer, the fermentation is more violent, and the holes left in the cheese are larger.

The length of curing time, and the manner in which the cheese is treated during this critical stage, differs so greatly from one cheese to another it would be impossible to describe them all. And it is during this period that little microorganisms in the atmosphere attach themselves to the cheese, creating in each case a unique flavor. Why should Pont l'Évêque cheese be so different from Brie, when both are soft cheeses made in the same region of the same country, presumably with milk from cows of the same breed? Because in the days when each of these cheeses originated, it was the practice always to use caves or deep underground cellars for curing, and the microorganisms in one cave would be of another species entirely from those in another.

This mystery of nature has not always been appreciated. The story of Liederkranz is an example. The cheese, originated by a delicatessen man in New York, Emil Frey, became so popular that it was decided to enlarge the operation and establish a factory in the dairy country of Ohio. A spotless new factory was built, everything was utterly hygienic, and the first lot of cheese was produced, faithfully following the old proven formula. But the resulting cheese was bland and uninteresting, not at all the same. Distressed, the manufacturer tried one improvement after another, without success. Only when the bacteria-infested wooden shelves were brought from the original factory and the mold on them scraped from the wood, to be smeared over the nice, hygienic walls of the new curing room, did their ripened Liederkranz taste as it had before.

It is also due to such microbes that one soft cheese will have a creamy white crust, another's crust will be reddish, still another will have an ocher-yellow rind. For centuries it was believed that the only way to maintain the particular characteristics of a cheese would be to cure it in the very same cave or cellar year after year. Now, of course, the cultures are isolated to be inoculated in the new cheese at the moment desired.

As the shaped cheese lies in the curing room, it must be turned over repeatedly so that air will reach all sides. This is just as true of the giant wheels of Swiss or natural Gruyère or Cheddar as of tiny, soft cheeses. And only the cheese maker can determine when the particular cheese has completed the curing stage and is ready to be ripened—a process that may take anywhere from two weeks to six months to several years. Cheeses that are semifirm when young gradually become very firm or even hard with aging, and may change color and flavor as well as texture. However, the bright yellow color of certain cheeses is due to an additive; this is not the cheese's natural color.

When a cheese is flavored with spices or herbs—caraway, cumin, sage, thyme, black pepper, paprika, and so forth—these are usually added before the shaped cheese is put out to cure. Other cheeses are flavored after curing, by pressing crushed grape pits, charcoal ash, red pepper, or paprika into the crust, or by wrapping them in vine leaves. Some cheeses form their own rinds as they ripen; others are deliberately wrapped with wax-coated cheesecloth, or rubbed with wax.

Some cheeses are cured in brine, cider, or white wine. This of course affects their flavor, as well as keeping them soft and acting as a preservative.

NATURAL VS. PASTEURIZED PROCESS CHEESE

Increasingly, even in the bulk cheeses sold in supermarkets, the designation "natural" will be seen on many cheese labels. This means that the cheese was allowed to ripen in the natural way, as just described. But most of the cheese produced for everyday use in this country is pasteurized—which is *not* the same as natural cheese made from pasteurized milk.

All American cheese produced commercially is made from pasteurized milk; also, by law under the Food and Drug Act, all imported cheeses must be made of pasteurized milk, with the exception of goat cheeses and Swiss-type cheeses (Emmentaler and natural Gruyère). Goat milk is not subject to the same disease-carrying bacteria that may enter cow's milk, and the process of making the big wheels of Swiss cheese is deemed sufficient to kill any such bacteria.

Actually, many cheese lovers contend that raw milk makes much better-flavored cheese than pasteurized milk, and that the harmful milk bacteria are eliminated anyway in the curing process. The semifirm and firm cheeses are especially safe. However, the demand for sterilization being what it is, the pasteurizing of milk reassures the wary, so the law must be observed.

It should be mentioned at this stage that when you take a cheese from the refrigerator and see that a blue mold has formed around the outside, the cheese is not spoiled. Cut away the mold and the cheese will still be perfectly safe for eating.

"Pasteurized process" cheese, by contrast, is made with two or more kinds of young (not aged) natural cheese, ground together into fine particles, then heated to a temperature of 400 degrees F., to a molten, homogenous plastic mass. The mixture is held at that temperature for between thirty seconds and five minutes, then cooled to room temperature and poured into waiting waxed cartons or plastic containers, which are instantly sealed hermetically.

From this point on, the cheese will no longer be able to ripen or change further. To connoisseurs, this sterilized plastic product has a rubbery texture and little character. But it will keep almost indefinitely under refrigeration, making it much easier to merchandise and allowing it to serve a useful pantry-shelf life in the kitchen.

Most of the world's cheese-making countries now process at least part of their output in this manner. A process cheese may be made soft, semisoft, or semifirm, and be molded into any shape desired. Much of it is molded into easily sliced loaf shapes, then it is pre-sliced and plastic wrapped in bulk, ready to ship to supermarkets.

Headquarters of N. Dorman & Co., Inc., at Syosset, New York. It is one of the largest producers, importers and distributors of cheese in the United States.

Cylindrical shaped cheese has been prepared by Dorman and is ready to be cut and packaged.

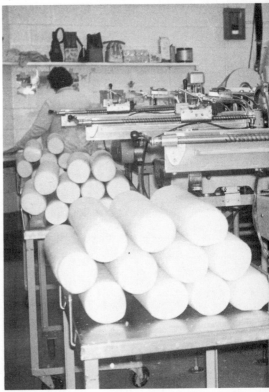

This festive display includes Roquefort, Pyramide, La Grappe, Port du Salut, Boursin, Bon Bel, Sainte-Maure (log), Banon and Brie.

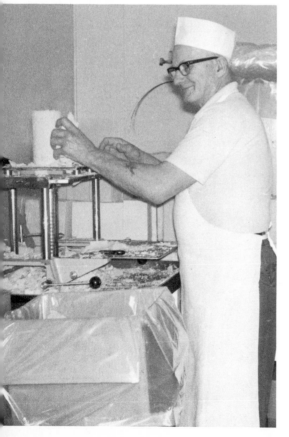

Bricks of cheese waiting to be trimmed and prepared before packaging. Trimmings are used in making processed cheese at Dorman.

Still another product of twentieth-century technical innovation is what is called "process cheese food," which may contain no more than 20 percent cheese, along with water, milk solids, whey, vegetable gum, and chemical preservatives. These are soft and easy to spread, and usually come in glass jars or plastic cups ready to put on the cocktail table. Some make very good eating indeed, even if calling them "cheese" is an exaggeration.

It's easy for the cheese snob to dismiss all pasteurized process cheeses contemptuously, but they fulfill the same need in modern living as the jug wines. As with wine drinking, it all depends on how sophisticated one's palate may be and what one is accustomed to. Those who have never known any other kind are quite content with the process cheeses, and the variety offered is certainly enormous, since they come in every size, shape, texture, type, and flavor.

A number of "gourmet cheeses"—chiefly soft cheeses, sometimes with three, four, or five cheeses blended together—are now also processed by pasteurizing. An example is Crème de Gruyère, velvety smooth, with a piquant but still delicate flavor. (The name Gruyère is so often given to process cheese, especially those produced in Switzerland and Denmark, that it is now necessary to distinguish the firm traditional cheese by calling it "natural Gruyère.") Very similar to Crème de Gruyère is a cheese called grappo or "grape cheese," which has crushed grape pits forming a crisp outer crust.

Another type of cheese to be found both in supermarkets and gourmet specialty shops are blends of cheese and wine, such as Cheddar in port or blue cheese in brandy. These are usually made of natural cheese to which the wine or brandy is added. They can be mixed up at home quite easily, even making use of bits and pieces of leftover cheeses for the purpose.

Just because a cheese carries the identification "natural" is not necessarily a mark of excellence. Much depends on whether the natural cheese has been ripened or aged sufficiently to have reached full maturity. Many supermarket Cheddars carry the notation "aged over six months." For a Cheddar, this is a minimum. And even when a cheese is excellent in its original wheel or loaf shape, pre-slicing robs it of much of its distinctive flavor. If you doubt this, make the experiment of comparing pre-sliced, pre-packaged cheese, such as Switzerland Swiss, with the same cheese cut fresh from the wheel and sliced just before eating.

THE LEADING FAMILIES OF CHEESE

In comparison with mastering wine technology, becoming knowledgeable about cheese is simple. Despite the hundreds of kinds of cheeses in existence (the cheese master at Calvert's Cheeserie in Washington, Tony Batista, told me he has accumulated a list containing names of eight hundred separate cheeses), all can be classified as belonging to one of the following seven "families."

The fresh unripened cheeses: Made simply of the pressed curds, no rennet. These include pot cheese, cottage cheese, cream cheese, quarg, ricotta, farmer cheese, and American Neufchâtel. Every cheese country has at least one, but they are too perishable for export.

The soft ripened cheeses: France excels in this category. Besides Camembert and Brie, there must be a hundred luscious such dessert cheeses made in France, each with its own subtly different flavor. The richest are those called *triple-crème*, carrying the highest amount of butterfat. Others not quite so rich are called *double-crème*.

Included in this "family" are Liederkranz, best of the American soft ripened cheeses, Crema Danica (from Denmark, of course), Italy's Bel Paese, and the Swiss Bel Lago (though this is sometimes semisoft).

The goat and ewe cheeses: So far none of these has been produced commercially in the United States, but the French goat cheeses have climbed so rapidly in popularity in the last few years that some enterprising cheese maker here may soon try to enter the field. The best known of the imported ewe cheeses (not including the blue ewe cheeses such as Roquefort) is feta, produced in several Balkan countries. Most of the French goat cheeses are soft or semisoft, chalky white, delicate yet tangy. These same adjectives could be used to describe many of the ewe cheeses, yet the flavor is quite different, and in texture, ewe cheeses tend to be smoother. Some ewe cheeses, however, when aged become hard enough to grate.

Semisoft cheeses: In this category, we can include Havarti, Port Salut, Pont l'Evêque, Bonbel, Crème de Gruyère, and Esrom. Sometimes it is hard to draw the line between a cheese classed as semisoft and one to be grouped as semifirm, since the consistency and texture differ from one cheese maker to another, and the length of time for ripening and aging will also make a difference.

Emmentaler, at Dorman, being cut into bricks to be sold at delicatessens.

A tempting assortment of eight cheeses make an attractive and tasty luncheon dessert, served with full-bodied red wine or a dessert wine. Far left, Colby; Swiss; front left, Edam, with Meunster alongside; Blue cheese, Caraway, Gouda and Camembert.

Semifirm cheeses: The Danes excel here. Somso, Tybo, and Danbo are three beautiful examples. American Muenster is sometimes semi-firm, as is brick. Another is the Welsh Caerphilly. Many cheeses are semifirm when young, become firm as they age; Monterey jack is such a cheese.

Firm to hard cheeses: In this category belong the Swiss-type big wheels, the Cheddar types (and there are more than eighty of these), and the Italian grating cheeses. Among the Swiss-type, include the Norwegian Jarlsberg, natural Gruyère, Blarney (from Ireland), and of course Emmentaler, the first. These are the cheeses that can be aged for years, usually becoming more firm to hard with time. Include also Edam, Gouda, Romano, Parmesan, provolone, caciocavallo, and hundreds of others in this great family.

The blue cheeses: Every cheese country has at least one of these. Most are inoculated with the *Penicillium roquefortii* culture, but others have their own unique mold. The blues range all the way from creamy and delicate (like Pipo Crem and the American Maytag) to sharp, flaky, and semifirm.

PAIRING CHEESE AND WINE

As a rule, mild or delicate-flavored cheeses are best with white wine, while the stronger cheeses go with red. But nearly *all* cheeses are good with red wine (with the exception of the very smelly ones).

The following listing attempts to describe each cheese, as well as to suggest in each case which wines go best with it, and vice versa. But just as wine preferences are highly personal, so are tastes in cheese, and inevitably, some will disagree with the combinations here suggested.

It must also be noted that the descriptions given are based on samples of the cheeses that I have personally tasted. But one encounters enormous variations in flavor and texture, depending on the individual manufacturer, the age of the cheese, and the way it has been stored. More than once I have been forced to reexamine my own original assessment of a cheese when later tasting a sample of another with the same name.

Whenever possible, ask to be given a tiny taste sample before buying any cheese. If the cheese is already packaged, such a request could not, of course, be honored. But the personnel in most cheese specialty shops are happy to give out slivers from wheels or loaves of cheese for the prospective buyer to nibble.

TIPS ON BUYING, SERVING, AND STORING CHEESE

Amounts of cheese to buy: Soft cheeses should *always* be purchased in small quantities. Whether ripened or unripened, their life span is short, and refrigeration can extend it only up to a point.

Firm cheeses, on the other hand, will remain good for months, especially if well wrapped, completely sealed. Some cheese men recommend brown paper as the best for wrapping. If this is a cheese you know and like, always buy at least one-half pound at a time, remembering that what's left over can be put away for another serving.

When you are exploring a cheese shop, buy "first tries" in the smallest quantity, to be sure you'll like them. Cheese is no longer an inexpensive food, and if the sample pleases you, you can always go back for more.

Ascertaining and assuring freshness: When buying an imported soft cheese, proceed with caution. It is wisest to buy these only from specialty cheese shops, where the turnover is large and the cheeses not so likely to have been lying overlong in the display cases. If the cheese should turn out to be overripe, you should always make a complaint. Any cheese that has a strong ammonial whiff when opened is already "gone."

Even those who proclaim they like "smelly cheeses, the smellier the better," surely don't mean to include in this category those that are suggestive of a grave robber's trophy. Yet there are some putrid-smelling cheeses, such as bierkäse, which apparently have a following or they wouldn't be manufactured and distributed so widely. *Chacun à son goût.*

Kinds of cheese to serve: When selecting cheese to be served with white or rosé wine, it's wisest when in doubt to stick to the very mild varieties. Very pungent, assertive cheeses need a robust red wine. The smellier ones aren't good with any wine; they belong with beer or cocktails.

Amounts to serve: How much cheese to figure on per serving for a party? It depends on what kinds and how many varieties of cheese you are buying, whether it's for a tasting, part of an hors d'oeuvres spread, or the prelude to a meal.

If nothing but cheese and wine are to be served, naturally you will serve more cheese than if there are to be other foods, too. Many cheeses can only be bought by the package, which may contain four

Cheeses by Borden, Inc., attractively arranged on a platter, enhanced by fruit and cherry tomatoes.

ounces, eight ounces, or even sixteen ounces (one pound). But when the cheese is being cut from a wheel and you are asked, "How much?" you must consider not only whether, say, one-half ounce per serving will be enough for your guests, but whether the wedge will look generous when set out on the serving table. As a host, it's better to be extravagant than stingy.

As a very, very rough rule of thumb, figure on one-half ounce per person for *each* cheese. This means, if you are offering four kinds of cheese to twenty persons, this will run to approximately five pounds of cheese altogether. But be sure to have plenty in reserve.

Crackers, bread, and such: The bland types are always preferable for a tasting, though for a wine and cheese party, such things as sesame crackers, rye crisps, and thin-sliced pumpernickel bread may be offered. For a serious tasting, French bread, or sourdough bread in long, thin loaves is considered the best. Indeed, nibbling on a piece of bread, unbuttered, is the best way to clear the palate in my estimation, better than taking a swallow of water.

How to serve: Arrange cheeses of different sizes and shapes on cheese trays, accompanied by a knife or knives for easy cutting. If you are having more than eight persons, better have the cheese in more than one place, to make it easier for guests to get at it. Put white wine cheeses on one table, red wine cheeses on another.

As with serving wine, the blander cheeses should be offered first, working up to cheeses with more assertive taste and aroma. But there are dozens of exceptions to this rule. It comes down really to a question of finesse.

Present a selection of cheeses that are different in texture as well as size and flavor. For example, one soft circular or wedge-shaped cheese, one semifirm loaf or wheel of cheese, and a third that is firm and can be sliced or cut into chunks or cubes.

Storing for short or long periods: A firm cheese need not be refrigerated at all if it is to be consumed within a week. In fact, it will have richer, fuller flavor if not refrigerated. But for a longer period it is probably best to store it in the refrigerator, well wrapped—as long as you remove it to room temperature an hour before serving.

Soft cheeses need refrigeration at all times, from the time of purchase until a few hours before serving. Can soft cheeses be frozen? The Department of Agriculture says yes, all kinds of cheese may be stored in the freezer. But I suspect that this explains why cheeses in supermarkets rarely have the same full flavor and moist texture of those purchased from a delicatessen or cheese specialty shop.

Freezing tends to dry out all foods, and cheese is bound to lose some of its normal moisture with freezing, which also causes it to be less creamy and velvety. Once a cheese has lost these qualities, bringing it back to room temperature cannot restore them.

Some refrigerators have special cheese storage compartments in the door where the temperature is not quite as cold as in the interior, on shelves. If yours has such a compartment, use it.

A GLOSSARY OF CHEESES
(AND THE WINES TO SERVE WITH THEM)

Appenzeller: From Switzerland, a firm cheese that is marinated in cider or white wine before aging. Of the same family as Emmentaler and natural Gruyère, but somewhat lighter, more moist and buttery, with a unique flavor, like a delicate version of Tilsit.

Wines: Dry to semidry whites, such as Riesling, Gewürztraminer, Pinot Chardonnay; also light red wines (claret, Beaujolais, Gamay).

Asiago: Originally a sharp-flavored, pale, firm Italian mountain cheese, hard enough to grate when aged. But an American cheese of this name is now being produced in New York State that is lighter, semifirm, with pungent flavor.

Wines: Full-bodied reds; the American version of the cheese may also be served with fruity semisweet whites.

Banon: *See* Chevret or Chevrotin.

Baton de Savoie: Small, round goat cheese with a crust of crushed grape pits; from Switzerland.

Wines: See Chevret or Chevrotin.

Beaumont: A soft to semisoft French cheese of the Camembert family.

Wines: Semidry white or light red.

Bel Lago: A soft to semisoft light, delicate cheese from Switzerland, a very good choice to serve with white wines.

Bel Paese: Creamy soft, light Italian dessert cheese with assertive flavor. Also made in Wisconsin under supervision of parent company.

Wines: Can be served with the heavier white wines (Montrachet, Sémillon, Sauternes) but is better with full-bodied red wines or tawny port, Madeira, or cream sherry.

Black Diamond: Canadian Cheddar, available in different sizes, in good distribution. Firm, sharp, but with a beautifully velvety texture, usually pale cream in color, but some is bright orange.

Wines: Red wines are best, especially the fuller-bodied, well-aged ones.

Blarney: *See* Emmentaler or Emmenthaler.

Bleu or Blue: As a generic name, this covers many, many different cheeses, made in every cheese country and in several American states, including North Carolina, Ohio, Wisconsin, Vermont, and Minnesota. *See also* bleu de Bresse, Danish blue, Gorgonzola, Mycella, Roquefort, Stilton, Maytag.

Wines: It's always safe to serve red wine and blue cheese together, especially a full-bodied red wine. But some of these also pair beautifully with tawny port, Madeira, or amontillado sherry.

Bleu de Bresse: A cheese made in Burgundy, very light creamy texture, but with sharper flavor than one expects from its appearance. Should be left at room temperature until so soft it is almost runny before serving. A popular brand name is Pipo Crem.

Wines: Full-bodied or tart red.

Bolina: A new blue cheese from Denmark, much creamier than Danablu. It can be described as a cross between Gorgonzola and Bleu de Bresse.

An all-Danish cheese platter offers Esrom, White Cream Cheese, Danish Blue, Danish Saint Paulin and Danish Brie. The tasty looking wedges are Danish Camembert, dipped in egg white and bread crumbs and fried in hot oil.

Wines: See Bleu or Blue.

Bonbel: A process French cheese available in wedges, with a light, smooth texture and mild flavor, not a distinguished cheese but easy to take, a good choice for a mixed group. A cheese by this name is now also made in New York State.

Wines: Light red wines, semidry white wines or rosé, also semisweet sparkling wines.

Bondost: Firm Swedish cheese sometimes flavored with cumin or caraway; also made in Wisconsin.

Wines: Red wines of any type; also semisweet or fruity white wines.

Boursault: *Triple-crème,* soft ripened French cheese, one of the most expensive and most elegant of the world's dessert cheeses.

Wines: Brut or sec champagne, semisweet white wines, amontillado sherry or tawny port.

Boursin: Soft, light French *triple-crème* cheese, chalky white. Some are pepper coated, others flavored with garlic or herbs. The plain Boursin no longer seems to be available in American shops. (For a low-cost substitute for Boursin, flavor cream cheese with black pepper and a bit of cayenne, and if you like, a dash of curry powder.)

Wines: The cheese flavored with garlic or herbs is not suitable to serve with wines, though it is a good appetizer cheese, to be offered with aperitif wines or cocktails. The pepper-coated Boursin will go well with semidry white wines or dry to semidry rosés. This and the spiced variation can both be offered with vermouth cocktails and dry sherry.

Brick: Pale golden, natural, semifirm American cheese molded in brick shape. More pungent aroma and softer texture than Cheddar. A delicious Danish cheese called Danish brick can also be found in many supermarkets. *See* Dofo Danish Brick.

Wines: Semidry or semisweet white wines, rosé, or light red wines.

Brie: One of the world's great cheeses, universally liked. Very delicate flavor, soft pale gold between white crusts. As sold in American shops, it is blander and more firm than in France, where it is considered not fit to serve unless runny soft and with distinctive taste and aroma. Some Bries are now being made in other countries, but none quite comes up to the French original.

Wines: Vintage or premium red wines, full-bodied, with generous bouquet. The blander Bries also go with soft or fruity white wines, semisweet to sweet, or with brut to demi-sec champagnes or medium to sweet (cream) sherries.

Brindza: A chalky white sheep cheese sometimes cured in brine (like feta) or pressed between layers of pine bark, which gives it a resinous flavor. Imported from Czechoslovakia and other Balkan nations; a version is also made in California.

Wines: Soft, light white wines or light reds.

Cabricetta: An Italian goat cheese. There is also a French goat cheese called "cabricette."

Wines: See Chevret or Chevrotin.

Caciocavallo: Firm, with buttery texture, has brownish rind acquired by hanging from rafters to age. Reminiscent of provolone in flavor but more delicate. Similar cheeses are made in several Balkan countries where the spelling may be "kashkaval," "kachavely," or some other combination.

Wines: Tart, assertive red wine, or very dry white wine.

Caerphilly: Very pale or creamy white, semifirm Welsh cheese with mild but distinctive flavor.

Wines: Almost any red or white table wine. This is also one of the few cheeses good with rosé and may be served with moderately dry sherry.

Caljak: A Massachusetts version of Monterey jack, delicate in flavor, semifirm, creamy even when taken direct from the refrigerator. Sold in sticks in many supermarkets.

Wines: See Monterey jack.

Camembert: The original has been made in the French town of this name since the twelfth century. The domestic French version is much more pungent in flavor and aroma than the cheeses of the same name (including the French imports) now available in American markets. The Danish Camembert is still milder and somewhat firmer, suitable to serve either as an appetizer or a dessert cheese. Some Bries and some Camemberts now seem very much alike, though traditionally Brie is supposed to be the more delicate of the two. The German Camembert is sometimes served with chopped onion and freshly ground pepper, to be spread on pumpernickel as an appetizer.

Wines: All red wines are good with Camembert, as are the dry or semi-dry whites. Like Brie, it is also a perfect cheese with champagne or with dessert wines.

Cantal: A semifirm to firm cheese produced in what is now the department of Cantal in the Haute Auvergne region of France. It is pale in color, with very tiny holes, and has a surprisingly tart flavor difficult to describe.

Wines: Surprisingly, this goes well with a very tart white wine, though it is usually recommended as proper to serve with light or tart red wines.

Caraway Cheddar: There are many Cheddar types containing caraway seeds, but this name usually means the pasteurized process cheese that may or may not be pre-sliced, and that often comes in rectangular shapes easy for cutting into cubes. Not a gourmet cheese, but suitable for serving to a mixed group.

Wines: Can be served with any *vin ordinaire,* red or white, but especially red.

Carré de l'Est: Another of France's soft ripened dessert cheeses, this one from the Champagne district. It's rich and light, somewhat resembling both Brie and Camembert, but not quite like either.

Wines: Not surprisingly, this is beautiful with champagnes or any other sparkling wines. Also with light fresh reds such as Beaujolais or the semidry rosé wines.

Chabichou or **Chavichou:** *See* Chevret or Chevrotin.

Chantelle: The commercial name of a blue cheese from Illinois.

Wines: See Bleu or Blue.

Chaource (pronounced "shurss"): A soft ripened French cheese similar to Brie.

Wines: See Brie.

Cheddar: Of the more than eighty cheeses that belong to this family, the best are the well-aged natural cheeses in large wheels that are usually quite sharp in flavor, though they range from mild and semifirm to very sharp and hard, and there are even semisoft Cheddars. Some pasteurized process cheese is also called Cheddar, and may be sold pre-sliced wrapped in plastic. *See also* Black

A full-bodied red Zinfandel, served with cheese and fruit, make a tempting and satisfying dessert.

Ideas for serving Zinfandel or Port, accompanied by various types of cheese, bread and crackers.

Diamond, Colby, Coon, Cooper, Dunlop, Gloucester, Herkimer County, Vermont Sage, and Vermont white Cheddar.

Wines: Full-bodied reds are best, especially for the sharper, firmer Cheddars. The lighter, milder types, especially those that are semi-firm, may, however, be served with white or rosé wines.

Cheshire: An English cheese, firm, piquant, but milder than most Cheddars, usually bright yellow in color (called "red Cheshire") but also may be pale, almost white, or "blue," meaning veined with the *Penicillium roquefortii* culture.

Wines: Goes well with semisweet rosés but is best with full-bodied or assertive reds. May also be served with sherry or other aperitif wines.

Chevret or **Chevrotin:** The generic name for all French goat cheeses, many varieties of which are now coming into this country and becoming ever more popular, as they well deserve. All are chalky white and creamy to flaky in texture, with mild yet piquant flavor. Some are tiny rounds that could fit in the palm of the hand and that may be covered with vine leaves or a blue-brown mold or crushed grape pits. Others, like Montrachet (q.v.), are in long rolls, which may be cut crosswise in circles to serve. Still others are in drum-shaped rounds that may be cut in wedges.

Wines: Full-bodied red wines are especially good with all the chevrets, the heavier Mediterranean reds, and the assertive Bordeaux types. But the delicate-flavored cheese may also be served with a semidry rosé or with semidry to semisweet whites, and is delicious with sparkling wines.

Chiberta: A Tomme de Pyrénées cheese with assertive flavor and light spongy texture, semifirm. "Tomme" means simply a mountain cheese, made usually by shepherds.

Wines: Dry to semidry white, or tart, assertive reds.

Colby: Firm, mild, natural Cheddar produced in Vermont, now in supermarket distribution in eight-ounce rectangular pieces plastic wrapped.

Wines: Almost any, but the cheese is recommended particularly to accompany white or rosé wines. It's one of the few Cheddars that goes well with these.

Comté: Firm French cheese similar to natural Gruyère, ivory yellow with medium-sized holes, usually of great size and legendary keeping qualities.

Wines: Especially recommended for white and rosé wines, though also good with any red wine.

Coon: A natural Cheddar now distributed by Kraft in four- and eight-ounce packages. The supermarket versions have much less character than the original, which used to be one of the really fine American Cheddars. Wheels of Coon are sometimes sold in delicatessens or cheese specialty shops, and these taste like a different cheese entirely.

Wines: Best with red wines.

Cooper: A milder Cheddar made in Vermont. Also available in supermarkets in plastic wrap.

Wines: See Cheddar.

Coulommiers: Of the Brie-Camembert family of soft ripened dessert cheeses, this is thicker than Brie and sold in round wooden hoops. When young and fresh, it is very soft, with the consistency of butter and a slight almond flavor. When fully ripened and older, its flavor becomes stronger and the texture firmer.

Wines: Light, fruity reds, semidry rosé wines, or medium to sweet sherry.

Crema Danica: Very rich, *triple-crème,* soft ripened dessert cheese from Denmark.

Wines: Light reds, rosé, semisweet to sweet white wines, brut to demi-sec champagne; also good with sparkling burgundy or Asti Spumante.

Crème de Gruyère: An imported light, semisoft process cheese of pale cream color. Spreads easily, and has a flavor faintly reminiscent of natural Gruyère, but more delicate.

Wines: Moderately dry to semisweet white or rosé or light red wines; also a good choice with sparkling wines.

Danbo: A variation of Danish Samso.

Danish blue or **Danablu:** The sharpest of the European blue cheeses, varying in quality and consistency according to the size of the package and length of time it has been in storage. Available in all supermarkets, but for a far better sample, have it cut from the wheel at a cheese specialty shop. Those who find it oversharp may like it better if spread over a base of unsalted butter on French bread. *See* also Bolina and Mycella.

Wines: Full-bodied, rather assertive red wines, preferably a vintage wine four or five years old.

Dofo Danish Brick: A velvety semifirm cheese with small irregular holes, piquant flavor.

Wines: Good with almost any wine; suitable for whites or rosé.

D'Oka or **Oka:** A Canadian soft to semisoft ripened cheese made by Trappist monks, pungent, aromatic, not to everyone's taste.

Wines: Full-bodied or tart red wines.

Dunlop: A beautiful Scottish Cheddar, very pale in color, firm, with sharp flavor but more velvety texture than most Cheddars.

Wines: Robust red wines.

Edam: The world-famous cannonball cheese of Holland, with red wax rind and mild yellow interior, now being produced in the United States and other countries, too; even France has one. Universally popular and versatile.

Wines: Goes well with almost any wine—dry red, white, and rosé—and also good with moderately dry to cream sherry, with port, Madeira, or other dessert wines.

Emmentaler or **Emmenthaler:** The original big-holed cheese of Switzerland, widely copied everywhere else. Germany, Austria, France, and Denmark all make a cheese they call Emmentaler (or Emmenthaler). The Irish call their version Blarney; we call ours Swiss (q.v.). In this country, Emmentaler is sold as "Switzerland Swiss," and the genuine cheese must always have this name on the label, stamped in red.

Wines: Almost every wine goes with Emmentaler, but it is particularly useful as a white wine cheese. For picnics, however, Emmentaler and red wine make a perfect pair.

Esrom: A velvety, semisoft Danish cheese with buttery consistency and edible rind, of the Port Salut family.

Wines: Good with fruity white or red wines.

Feta: The milk-white sheep cheese of the Balkans. The brine in which it is cured is responsible for its piquantly salty flavor. The Bulgarian feta is both creamier and firmer than the others; the Yugoslav, more salty and sharp; the Greek version, the best known and most available, is semisoft and piquant without being overly salty.

Kraft Kitchens present an eye-catching assortment of their cheeses: cubes of Medium Cheddar to the left; Sharp Cheddar cut in wedges; and sliced Longhorn Style Colby, placed against a festive Christmas background.

Variety is the keynote in this wine and cheese tasting setup, with both red and white wine and firm and soft cheeses.

Feta is now available, imported from Greece, in some supermarkets in jars, though the texture is better if purchased fresh from the barrel in a Greek-American delicatessen. There is also a Danish feta in some supermarkets. (The Danes seem to enjoy making their version of almost every known cheese of the world.)

Wines: Light red wine, or soft, fruity white wine.

Fontina: A bright yellow, semisoft cheese, originally produced in Italy, where it's a stronger-flavored cheese than the versions now being made in Sweden, Denmark, and France. A "white fontina" is also made in the United States.

Wines: An especially good choice to serve with white or rosé wines, though the stronger Italian versions are best with red.

Fontinella: Not in the least like fontina, the name is a puzzle. It's a Wisconsin cheese, probably produced by Italian-Americans, for it is nearly always available in delicatessens specializing in Italian foods. A beautiful, firm cheese, light in color, flaky, with exquisite flavor—worth searching out.

Wines: Best with red wines, though it can also be served with a rather heavy or fruity white wine. Not recommended for rosé.

Gervais: Another of the beautiful, soft ripened French dessert cheeses, not quite as rich in butterfat as Boursault or Brie, but like softened butter in consistency, with a very delicate flavor.

Wines: Champagne, Moselle, or a well-balanced soft, dry white wine such as Wente Brothers Le Blanc de Blancs.

Gloucester: An English Cheddar with firm, velvety texture and beautiful flavor, not too sharp.

Wines: Any red wine.

Gorgonzola: Italy's blue cheese, whose veining is really green. When young it is creamy soft and delicate, but when fully ripened and older it becomes much stronger and a little brown around the edges.

Wines: Like all blue cheeses, Gorgonzola is best with red wines, the more robust the better.

Gouda: Like Edam, this is of Dutch origin and frequently manufactured in the same round shape with red wax exterior. Usually it is larger than Edam and may be in the shape of a loaf, with a golden rather than red rind. There is also a vintage Gouda, aged for several years, a connoisseur's choice. Smoked Gouda may or may not be a process cheese; usually small, with a red wax rind, this variation is more of an appetizer item than a wine cheese.

Wines: See Edam.

Gourmandise: A buttery soft process French cheese, flavored with kirsch, that melts in the mouth. Everyone, young and old, will like it.

Wines: An excellent dessert cheese to go with all white wines, dessert wines, or as a spreading cheese on delicate wafers. A good choice with wine punches or sparkling wines, and beautiful with ruby or tawny port, rosé wines, or the heavier pink or kosher wines.

Green Mountain jack: A Vermont version of the jack that originated in California, produced by the Sugarbush cheese makers, all of whose cheeses are noteworthy. A versatile cheese, can be served with any wine.

Gruyère: So many process cheeses and cheese foods now carry this name, it has become necessary to call the original firm, big-wheeled cheese "natural Gruyère," to distinguish the difference.

The natural Gruyère is made by much the same method as Emmentaler but has a higher proportion of butterfat and smaller holes (and some have no holes at all). Its texture is somewhat softer than that of Emmentaler, though still quite firm. This is the perfect cheese for making fondue, in combination with Emmentaler (or Swiss) and perhaps a bit of Cheddar. Also versatile as a snack or sandwich item.

The process Gruyère cheeses, many of which are made in Switzerland and others in Denmark, are usually sold in round boxes containing individually wrapped wedges. Some of these are flavored with spices, herbs, or wine. *See also* Crème de Gruyère.

Wines: Natural Gruyère is perfect with all white and rosé wines, also good with reds, and with sherries, Madeira, champagne, what you will.

Havarti: A delicate and delicious semisoft to semifirm cheese from Denmark, made in the town of this name for over a hundred years, now available in plastic packaging in supermarkets. One version contains caraway seeds. Buttery smooth, lovely flavor. But supermarket Havartis are sometimes overfirm and less flavorful, apparently because of long, too-cold refrigeration.

Wines: Like Edam, this will go with almost any wine.

Herkimer County: Another New York Cheddar, sharp, flaky, so pale it's almost white, with a black wax-treated cheesecloth cover. Improves greatly in flavor with aging.

Wines: Red wines, especially the more full-bodied types.

Jack: *See* Monterey jack.

Jarlsberg: A firm, pale yellow Norwegian cheese with small and large holes, belonging to the family of Swiss cheeses, with a flavor somewhat like natural Gruyère but more delicate and softer in texture. Very versatile, delicious, and available in many American supermarkets.

Wines: *See* Emmentaler.

Kashkaval: The Balkan version of caciocavallo, but may be in a loaf or wheel instead of ball shape. The name is spelled in several ways, according to the country. The Yugoslav version is more pungent than the Hungarian, and the Bulgarian version stronger than the Yugoslav. All are delicious, with that faintly smoky taste something like provolone.

Wines: Best with simple, young red wines, but can also be served with semidry or semisweet whites.

Kasseri: A semifirm to firm cheese made in Greece and Yugoslavia. It has a salty piquancy, is a good appetizer cheese, and is often cubed and fried in deep fat or hot olive oil to be served as a hot hors d'oeuvre.

Wines: Light dry white, rosé, or red wines.

Lappi: A Finnish cheese, firm, with flavor like Swiss, but no holes. Made with skimmed milk.

Wines: Good with white or rosé.

Liederkranz: Not as available as it should be, this soft ripened American cheese is unique. When fresh and young (the crust should be beige to light ocher, not the least brownish) it is pungent but velvety. If overripe it becomes ammoniac. Probably in short supply because it is so perishable. The cheese was originally named after the choral society of which its inventor, Emil Frey, was a member at the time.

Wisconsin Dairies at Richland Center, Wisconsin, manufactures between 25 and 30 million pounds of cheddar cheese a year. The cheese "starter" is made in 800-gallon tanks, such as this one pictured.

One of eight huge "make vats" at Wisconsin Dairies. The size of the vat gives an idea of the enormity of an operation capable of manufacturing 142,500 pounds of cheddar daily —a far cry from the way farmers once made their own cheddar in simple wooden vats.

Wines: Red wines of any type, but especially clarets.

Liptauer: Sometimes found as a process cheese, pale in color and very creamy, though the original Austrian sheep cheese is a ripened cheese, white and crumbly. A popular hors d'oeuvres cheese mixture is also called by this name.

Wines: Red wines or rosé.

Longhorn: A natural Cheddar made in Wisconsin, now distributed by Kraft.

Wines: Best with red wines.

Manteca: An Italian variation of provolone, with sweet butter placed in the center when the cheese is set out to ripen. Less firm than provolone.

Wines: See Provolone.

Maytag: One of the most admired of American blues, produced and marketed by the manufacturers of Maytag washing machines! This is a very creamy, soft blue, one many people prefer because of its mild flavor.

Wines: See Bleu or Blue.

Monterey jack: Of California origin, this can be a beautiful cheese, the young jack semifirm, very delicate and velvety, the older cheese more deeply yellow, firmer, zestier. Unfortunately, it is now being mass produced, and while still a natural cheese, most supermarket versions do not do it justice.

Wines: Almost any wine—white, rosé, or red—dry to semidry sherry, vermouth, sparkling wines, etc.

Montrachet: Made in the same district of Burgundy as the renowned white wine of this name, this is a superb goat cheese shaped in a long roll, the outside covered with charcoal ash. It will remain fresh much longer than the soft ripened cheeses if kept under refrigeration. Some people eat the charcoal covering with the cheese. Personally, I prefer it without. It needs to be spread on crisp, bland crackers or French bread.

Wines: Not surprisingly, the cheese is beautiful with Montrachet wine —or with any semidry white wine. The red Burgundy types of wine are also excellent with it. *See also* Chevret or Chevrotin.

Morbier: A semifirm sheep cheese made by shepherds in the high peaks of the Jura Mountains, easy to recognize because there is a line of gray ash running down the center. This is because the cheese is cured in shallow pans over the heat of charcoal fires and the ash from the fire settles over the top of the cheese. When two panfuls of cheese are put together to ripen, face to face, the line of ash remains inside. A mild, semifirm cheese with distinctive flavor.

Wines: Red wines, preferably the more robust types; some semidry whites.

Muenster or Münster: The American cheese of this name bears no relation to the Muenster made in Alsace, Denmark, or Germany, where it is a round, semisoft, rather smelly cheese. The American cheese is firm, brick- or square-shaped, with delicate flavor. It sometimes has tiny holes, sometimes is smooth and solid in texture. At its best, this is one of our finest cheeses, but some of the samples sold plastic-wrapped in supermarkets are quite the opposite. Always try to buy it in a cheese specialty shop or delicatessen, cut especially to your order—and ask for a sliver to sample first.

Wines: The European Muenster is best with a fruity or spicy wine, such as a Sylvaner or Gewürztraminer. The American Muenster, at its best, makes a very fine cheese to serve with white wine, though it is also good with reds, of course.

Muetschli: A melting cheese from Switzerland, where it is used primarily to make the popular dish Raclette, in a Raclette stove or table unit. (The cheese is sometimes sold under the name Raclette.) It can be eaten in chunks, but is better melted. The softened cheese is scraped off as it melts from the heat of the stove. Usually served in Switzerland as a supper snack with boiled potatoes and dill pickles. Also sold under the name Raclette.

Wines: Very dry or fruity white wines such as Gewürztraminer, Sylvaner, Riesling, or Neuchâtel, the Swiss white wine.

Mycella: A blue cheese from Denmark, much milder and creamier than Danish Blue, and its mold is more green than blue in color.

Wines: See Bleu or Blue.

Neufchâtel: In France, this is a soft ripened cheese with delicate flavor, much like a Petit Suisse. In the United States it means a fresh unripened cheese, like ordinary cream cheese in appearance, but with lower butterfat. Now sometimes sold as a cold pack cheese blended with blue cheese, a pasteurized process appetizer item.

Wines: Wine punches or semisweet white or rosé wines.

Petit Suisse: Very delicate and rich, a *double-chème* soft ripened cheese from France, served primarily for dessert, accompanied by strawberries or other fresh fruit.

Wines: Any dessert wine.

Pont l'Evêque: A Normandy cheese of the Port Salut family but very odoriferous.

Wines: Too strong for any but a quite heavy red wine—and it could kill the flavor of a good wine.

Pipo Crem: *See* Bleu de Bresse.

Port Salut: A cheese originally made by Trappist monks in France but now made in many countries and by cheese makers who have no connection with the monastic order. Some cheeses of this name are very delicate, almost too bland in flavor, others can be quite pungent. All are soft to semisoft. Saint-Paulin (q.v.), Reblochon (q.v.), D'Oka (q.v.), and Pont l'Évêque (q.v.) belong to the same family, but are considerably stronger and more smelly.

This operation shows how salt is added to a finishing table of cheese.

Cheese coagulating in a "make vat" in the foreground. Below is a finishing table of cheese.

Any Port Salut that has an ammoniac odor is overripe and should be returned to the cheese shop—or thrown out.

Wines: The more delicate ones are perfect to serve with white wines of any type. The smellier ones need a red wine.

Provolone: The Italian original is a smoked cheese with a heavy brown rind, firm to hard, with a distinctly smoky flavor. The cheeses of this name now made in the United States are semifirm to firm, milder in flavor, and easier to slice. For best flavor, buy it in a cheese specialty shop, an Italian delicatessen, or a corner grocery. The supermarket versions, especially those sold pre-sliced, like all mass-produced cheeses, have lost most of their original character, although they are still a good choice to serve to a mixed group, especially when it's the kind of affair when make-your-own sandwich materials are set out.

Wines: The cheese is good with both white and red wines, but if there's a choice, the red wine is preferable.

Reblochon: French semisoft cheese of Port Salut family.

Wines: See Port Salut.

Roquefort: Sometimes called "the king of cheeses and the cheese of kings," Roquefort is one of the world's great cheeses, made with the milk of ewes, inoculated with the *Penicillium roquefortii* culture, originally ripened in the high mountain caves of the Roquefort region but now in cellars where similar conditions are maintained. A red sheep always appears on the package label. While it is sold everywhere already packaged in four-ounce and eight-ounce wedges, you'll do better to buy it cut to your order at a cheese specialty shop.

Wines: Red wines only, according to the French, should be offered with Roquefort, though I like it also with tawny port.

Sage: A Cheddar cheese flavored with sage before curing, made in England and in Vermont. The sage gives the cheese a slightly green color. Sage is also sometimes added to cream cheese or Neufchâtel.

Wines: This is an appetizer rather than a wine cheese, but could be served with red wine.

Saint-Germain: A soft ripened French cheese formed into a three-inch round, very buttery, delicate, exquisite flavor.

Wines: See Coulommiers.

Saint-Marcellin: A goat cheese wrapped in vine leaves.

Wines: See Chevret.

Saint-Nectaire: A firm, aged goat cheese from the Auvergne, more assertive in flavor than the soft white goat cheeses, and firmer in texture.

Wines: Calls for crisp, dry wine, white or red.

Saint-Paulin: *See* Port Salut.

Samso: A lovely Danish cheese, pale gold, creamy, mild in flavor, available in smallish wheels (about twelve inches) or in a larger loaf shape.

Wines: Light red or fruity white or rosé.

Serra Curada: An aged version of Serra de Estrella that is semifirm to firm with a crust liberally sprinkled with paprika. It has a piquant spicy flavor, an excellent appetizer cheese.

Wines: Best with a tart or assertive red; also with aperitif wines.

Serra de Estrella: A cheese rarely seen here but worth looking for. A sheep cheese from the Estrella mountains of Portugal, cured with

Unloading a table of cheese by blowing it into giant barrels.

rennet from a thistlelike plant, molded in round wheels about twelve inches in diameter and two inches thick. Most esteemed when so runny it burst its ocher-colored rind and flows out. Flavor is sometimes tart, sometimes mellow. Quite unique.

Wines: Good with either a smooth, robust red wine, or a fruity semidry white.

Stilton: Perhaps England's greatest contribution to the world of gastronomy, a truly magnificent blue cheese that melts in the mouth. Only someone utterly dull of soul could fail to be inspired by it. Until recently it had never been imitated elsewhere, but now the Sugarbush cheese factory in Vermont has dared make a "Stilton-bleu," which as a copy is not bad, but to compete with the English original is impossible.

Wines: Traditionally in England this should be accompanied by a vintage or crusted port, though any good Portuguese tawny port is fine with it, as is any full-bodied red wine. It also makes a very fine appetizer cheese with cocktails.

Swiss: The American big-holed cheese originally made in Wisconsin by Swiss immigrants pursuing the same techniques as their forebears in Switzerland. Now an American classic; some truly memorable natural Swiss cheeses are being made in several American states. A decent Swiss, like a decent Cheddar, should be aged a minimum of six months, better up to a year or more. Unfortunately, "Swiss" can also mean a pre-sliced process cheese, which will do for lunch box sandwiches, but . . . even the best of the Swiss cheeses when pre-sliced and plastic wrapped lose character and finesse.

Wines: Swiss is a good choice for white wine, almost any white wine, including champagne. But it goes equally well with reds.

Syrian braided cheese: Now being made in Massachusetts, this curious cheese is literally braided, but when its wax covering is removed, it turns out to be quite soft, with a piquant flavor.

Wines: Full-bodied red wines are best, but the cheese is adaptable.

Taleggio: A creamy pale Italian dessert cheese with a red-hued crust, quite aromatic.

Wines: Port, Asti Spumante, and other semisweet to sweet sparkling wines or white dessert wines (Marsala, cream sherry) go well with this unique dessert cheese.

Telemi: Of Rumanian origin, where it is made of ewe's milk, an American cheese of the same name is semisoft to semifirm, so pale it is almost white, with a delicate but piquant flavor. More available in the West than the East.

Wines: Especially recommended for soft, dry, or semidry white or rosé wines.

Tilsit or Tilsiter: A pungent cheese, semifirm with small holes, made in Germany, Switzerland, several Scandinavian countries, and also the United States. Its flavor is almost too pungent for a wine cheese, but it may be served with a tart, assertive red.

Tomme: A generic term meaning "mountain cheese" in France. These vary greatly. Some are made of cow's milk, some with goat's or ewe's milk. *See also* Morbière, Chevret, Chiberta.

Tybo: A variation of Samso, also from Denmark.

Vermont sage: A sage Cheddar produced by the Sugarbush firm and widely available in cheese specialty shops.

Wines: Dry red, or, second choice, semidry whites.

Here, barrels are being filled with cheese on an assembly line.

Quality control—"plugs" of cheese are taken from barrels for testing.

Vermont white Cheddar: As the name implies, the color is so pale it's almost white, but the cheese is firm, flaky, and sharp in flavor.
Wines: Best with red.
Wensleydale: A superb firm, English Cheddar type, parchment colored, flaky, subtly pungent rather than sharp flavor, thick rind.
Wines: Full-bodied red wines, or ruby or tawny port.

Though you will never find a cheese by this name in a shop, "everlasting cheese" is one worth knowing about. This is made with the bits, pieces, and tag ends of almost any natural cheeses hanging around in the refrigerator. Grate hard or firm cheeses, or chop into small bits. Put into a blender with a little olive oil (a tablespoon of oil to a cup of cheese,) some butter (just enough to beat it to a smooth consistency), and a little bourbon or brandy. Even blue cheese can be blended with Cheddar, cream cheese, and tag ends of semisoft or semifirm cheeses. Beat until very smooth, then shape into a mold and cover with minced parsley. Or serve simply as a spread, with butter knives and crackers, or with thin-sliced pumpernickel. With red wine, this makes the best of snacks.

CHEESES AND THE CALORIES PROBLEM

One of the sad realities that cheese lovers must face is that nibbling at their favorite snack food can altogether wreck an otherwise conscientious dieting regime.

The only cheeses that are comparatively low in calories are the soft unripened or fresh cheeses, such as cottage cheese, farmer cheese, ricotta, and Neufchâtel. Not all cottage cheese is low in calories, however—it depends on the quantity of cream that has been added to it.

There are a number of firm natural cheeses made partially with skim milk that are somewhat less caloric than others. Include in this group most of the cheeses classified as in the Swiss or Emmantaler family, though not natural Gruyère, because its butterfat content is higher than that of its big-holed sister cheese. Other skim milk cheeses include Jarlsberg, Appenzeller, Bondost, provolone, the Finnish cheese called Lappi, and a few of the natural Cheddars. Usually (but not always) the firm-to-hard cheeses contain less butterfat than the soft ones. Read cheese labels: if made partially with skim milk, the label must say so.

The ones you can be sure are high in calories are the soft dessert cheeses, especially the French cheeses classified as *double-crème* or *triple-crème,* and our own cream cheese.

Most of the sheep and goat cheeses should be lower in butterfat because the milk itself is not as rich as cow's milk. However, those that seem creamy and light in texture probably contain more fat than the firmer, flakier ones.

The process cheese foods, such as the soft spreads sold in glass jars, and some of the packaged appetizer cheese products contain less butterfat because they contain proportionately so little cheese. Studying the labels of each of these will be enlightening. Remember that by law the ingredients must now be so listed as to give those in largest proportion at the beginning. If the second ingredient, for example, is water, and in the list you also see concentrated whey or nonfat dry milk solids, you can be reasonably sure that this is a cheese food comparatively low in calories. Vegetable gum is usually added to give the product spreadable texture, but I don't know whether anyone has yet figured out the calorie count of vegetable gum. It is primarily carbohydrate, but still should not contain as many calories as butterfat.

To make low-calorie cheese spreads or pâtés, or cheese balls, substitute farmer cheese, made mostly of skim milk, for cream cheese in recipes for these. Also, one or more of the process cheese foods may be blended with a real cheese (grated or shredded) for an interesting flavor combination. For example, combine Roka cheese food spread with grated Monterey jack or brick cheese. According to the ingredient list on the jar, Roka is made with Neufchâtel, a skimmed-milk cheese, blue cheese (obviously from the flavor a very, very small amount), water, condensed whey, dehydrated skim milk, vegetable gum, and artificial flavoring. Its calorie count must be fairly low, but the same must also be said of its flavor.

Recipes for a few low-calorie cheese tidbits are included in the final section of this book, under menus for tastings and parties.

HOST'S HAND BOOK

We might make a poem of saying the beauty of serving wine and cheese lies in its ease—but that would be only the opening couplet. There's poetry, too, in tasting and comparing.

Does the tingle of a Chardonnay on your tongue make you think of springtime? What words are best to describe the way a mellow Gorgonzola melts in your mouth? That "bramble" flavor sometimes remarked in a vintage Zinfandel—do you, too, find something about its aftertaste reminiscent of raspberries under a summer sun?

The best kind of party is one in which host and hostess enjoy themselves as much as their guests, and a wine and cheese tasting fills that requirement perfectly, because tasting, then comparing notes, is a game all can play. And this is the easiest kind of party to throw, for the only advance preparation consists of selecting the wines and the cheeses and putting them out on the table.

HOW MANY GUESTS TO INVITE

The smaller and more intimate the group, the more serious the tasting becomes. Not that it's essentially more difficult to offer cheese and wine to twenty or thirty persons instead of four to twelve, but with increasing numbers present, inevitably it becomes more of a social occasion and less of a strictly gourmet adventure—unless everyone has come especially to taste and compare, with a serious interest in learning more.

When I've attended big wine tastings, it often seems to me that most of the guests are drinking wine about as matter-of-factly as if they had highballs in their hands, and gossip and jokes dominate the conversation far more than gastronomic analysis. Not that they lack interest in the wines they are tasting, but social intercourse comes first. And the larger the group, the more likely that a sizable proportion of those present are not all that fascinated by exotic cheeses and unfamiliar wines.

So, in determining the number to invite, you are also deciding the kind of party it's to be. For a larger party, you will give more attention to such things as an attractive table setting, where to serve the wine and where the cheese, making sure traffic keeps flowing, whether special decorations are called for, even perhaps the question of introducing games or contests as added entertainment.

For a big bash, you may also have to rent glassware to have enough for everyone, and if it's an out-of-doors affair, you may want to put up a tent for the serving pavilion, and have an accordionist or guitarist wandering among the guests.

THE INVITATIONS

For a small group, invitation by phone is the easiest, and if these are old friends you are inviting, it can be spur of the moment, inspired perhaps by a visit to a cheese and wine shop where you got carried away and bought far more than you intended.

But for a larger gathering, printed party invitations and cards with a requested RSVP offer an advantage. You can fill in not only the day, time, and place, but perhaps even mention which wines and cheeses are to be offered. Now that wine and cheese parties have become so popular, specializing is bound to be the next step. You don't want your big wine and cheese tasting to be just like that given by a neighbor a few months ago, do you?

You may want to serve only sherries and other aperitif wines, and appropriate appetizer cheeses. Or you might want to make it an international tasting, with a selection of cheeses from many different countries, and a selection of accompanying wines from many countries as well. Or you might have a fondue supper, with a tasting of mostly white wines, with a red wine or two so your guests can decide which they like best with fondue, red or white wine.

Mail invitations at least two weeks in advance, so that you will know how many to expect, for that in itself may determine how much variety you will be able to offer.

Also, be firm about the time of starting—don't, for example, say "about five"—as everyone should be present before the tasting begins.

HOW MUCH TO BUY, HOW MUCH TO SPEND

Unless you set a limit in the beginning, you can find the cost of a wine and cheese party getting altogether out of hand. Some of the premium wines—not only imports, but the more epicurean American wines—now cost $3, $4, $5, and up to $8 a bottle—and more. Even supermarket cheeses cost from $1.00 to $2.50 a pound, and some more esoteric imported cheeses run far above this.

On the other hand, if you set your limit and stick to it, it is possible to offer a really excellent selection for a total outlay of between $2.50 and $3.00 per person—and remember that everyone is happy to learn about good, inexpensive wines.

Use a rule-of-thumb estimate of one-half bottle of wine and one-quarter pound of cheese per person, establish the number of bottles and pounds you will need, then see what can be worked out within a set price limit in each category. If one wine is an expensive one, balance the cost by choosing another in the lower price ranges. The same with cheese.

In those shops carrying both wines and a large assortment of cheeses under the same roof, you can turn with assurance to the manager or his party consultant for suggestions. The latter can also help you figure out how much you need of both wine and cheese to be sure of not running short, and advise you on which to choose in order to stay within your budget.

And remember that for an informal type of party, not strictly a tasting, the half-gallon and gallon-sized jugs and the magnums of European wines are economical.

Remember that fine wines should be delivered at least a day or two before your party. The wine can be left in the paper cartons, as long as the bottles lie on their side, not upright, in a reasonably cool place. This might be in your garage, if the weather is not too cold or too hot. The cheese, except for the soft ripened ones, need not be refrigerated; in fact, it's best not to put them in the refrigerator if they are to be served within thirty-six hours after delivery. Simply put them in a reasonably cool place, away from heat sources and sunlight, and protected from nibblers, either human or rodent. If you happen to have a wine cellar, that's a perfect place to keep both the wine and cheese.

Make sure all the cheese—including the soft ripened cheeses—is at regular room temperature for at least one hour before serving, and uncork all the red wines then, too. The white wines and sherry should not be refrigerated for more than one hour, the sparkling wines no more than two. If you don't have enough room in your refrigerator, the bottles can be placed in buckets with ice packed around them—either very small ice cubes or coarsely crushed ice, for about half an hour before serving, turning the bottles now and then so they chill uniformly. Sparkling wines must be thoroughly chilled, otherwise when the cork is drawn the wine will spill out in such a foam much of it will be lost. You could ask the wine merchant to chill the wine for you, then deliver it at the last moment.

GLASSWARE

Many hosts now serve red wine in the glasses shown at the left, white in the tulip-shaped six-ounce glass at the right; the tulip-shape, however, often referred to as "all-purpose," is suitable for any table wine—red, white, or rosé.

Much has been written about the proper stemware for serving the different kinds of wine. Today few people worry about having different glasses for different wines. The standard eight-ounce stemmed goblet will do for tasting any of the table wines—white, rosé, or red—and is also suitable for champagne.

For tasting, no more than two ounces should be poured in the glass, which means it will not be more than one-quarter full. However, to absorb the full beauty of a wine's bouquet, the taster should put his nose clear inside the glass, so that the rim touches the bridge of the nose, then breathe in deeply.

Even for serving wine at table, a wine goblet should not be filled more than half full, never more than two-thirds, in order to appreciate the bouquet.

There are three reasons why it makes a difference to serve wine in a clear stemmed goblet. First, holding up the goblet by the stem, the jewellike color and clarity of the wine can be observed. Then, if it's a red wine, the hand can be cupped around the bowl in such a way as to warm the wine and thus help to release the bouquet.

Conversely, with a white wine, when it should not be warmed, the stem is held only by the fingers; they should not touch the bowl itself.

Using the large tulip goblet for champagne or other sparkling wine is urged because the bubbles do not dissipate as quickly in the deeper bowl as in the saucer shape, and again the bouquet can be more fully appreciated. The saucer-shaped champagne glass may be more fun to use, but for tasting it is considered less practical.

For well-aged vintage red wines, some epicures insist on using "balloon" goblets, with almost twice the diameter and just as deep as the tulip-shaped, for fully savoring the wine's bouquet. These are not the same as large brandy snifters: they are as wide at the brim as the widest part of the bowl. These, too, should not be filled more than one-fourth full. If you happen to own such balloon glasses, by all means put them out, but don't feel you must buy them for the occasion.

Similarly, if you happen to have saucer-shaped champagne glasses, and want to use them for a sparkling wine tasting, your guests will certainly not mind. In fact, stemmed sherbet glasses may also be used for serving any sparkling wine.

For sherry, port, Madeira, or other sweet fortified wines (not the vermouths, however), the small, thinner four-ounce tulip shape is considered best. This is so much like a whiskey sour glass, you may use the latter if you have them. This is the glass used for serving sherry in Spain. It is preferable to the three-ounce fluted glass, for again, one can appreciate the bouquet better from the deeper tulip shape. But sherry, too, can be offered for tasting in a larger six- or eight-ounce tulip, if servings are kept small.

At a tasting, to serve any wine on the rocks, including dry sherry, is a paradox, because the ice waters the wine and kills its bouquet. But for a big party, where wines are not being tasted that critically, what are popularly called "old-fashioned glasses" will do quite nicely, especially for those who prefer their sherry on the rocks, no matter what the epicures say. Old-fashioned glasses also are just the thing for vermouth, or any of the herbal wines, which have no appreciable bouquet to be admired.

And suppose one doesn't have enough of the proper glassware for a party? Renting may be the best solution—if you can't borrow from close friends who will be coming. Rental services are listed in the yellow pages, and those advertising "party and banquet needs" are sure to be able to furnish you with wine and champagne glasses. Order half again to twice as many glasses as you will have guests, for, as at cocktail parties, empty glasses get put down and can't be found again.

What about plastic or paper cups? To a connoisseur, this is absolute

A "basic" stemware "wardrobe" is suggested above. The saucer-shaped champagne on the left may be used either as a sherbet (dessert) glass or for sparkling wine. Next is a popular shape either for red wine or for chilled Moselle or other dry white wine. The third is the all-purpose tulip-shape, and the glass on the right, a fluted champagne.

The "balloon burgundy" or over-sized wine glass shown on the left is fast growing in popularity; it is especially suitable for serving red table wine or sangría. The remaining two glasses are suitable, interchangeably, for either red or white wine, though for full appreciation of bouquet, the tulip-shaped glass (on the right) is preferable.

There is no rule that says wine glasses have to be of any specific shape or size and many enjoy these nineteenth-century styles in stemware. To enjoy the bouquet of a well-aged red wine, the glass in the center is preferable, filled only half full; that on the left is better for white wine, filled two-thirds full, and the glass on the right for dessert wine.

anathema. The plastic coating contributes its chemically-treated flavor to the wine, and any decent wine will cringe at being subjected to such an indignity. It's better to improvise with what you have, supplemented if necessary by borrowing from neighbors or some of the guests coming to the tasting. The proper shape is not as important as that it should be made of real glass, clear crystal, so that the wine's clarity may be viewed and neither taste nor bouquet adulterated with other flavors.

Cocktail glasses, sherbets of any size or shape, even juice glasses may come to the rescue. In fact, *vin ordinaire* tastes just as good from a juice glass as from any other, and is often served in thick tumblers in simple little European restaurants and cafés. It's not as elegant, but 'twill do. If you're giving a big informal party, or a tasting of good but inexpensive wines, line up the juice glasses and don't apologize.

TABLE SETTINGS AND ACCOMPANIMENTS

When a small, intimate gathering of friends has come to taste your wines and cheeses, the living room cocktail table is as good a place as any for displaying the selection. And there just isn't any "table setting" involved—except remembering to have a pile of cocktail-sized napkins handy and bread-and-butter plates for the cheese and breads.

But if more than a dozen are coming to your party or tasting, it becomes important to think of traffic. Then you put the wine and glassware on one table, the cheeses and breads on another. As a matter of practicality, either a paper or plastic-coated cloth should be laid over the wine table, for it's almost inevitable that some wine will be spilled before the evening is out. Red wine makes a miserable stain, and while white wine is not quite so lethal, it, too, can leave a yellowish mark. It's wise to have at least one well-filled salt cellar on hand for an emergency, in case someone should spill red wine on clothing. If the wine spot is immediately covered with salt, chances of its being washed out successfully later are pretty good. "Spray N' Wash," an aerosol spot remover, is also effective in removing wine stains from washable fabrics.

No such disposable cover is necessary for the cheese table, and you may find that the cocktail table will serve nicely for this purpose, if it's a large one. Or if yours is a show-off kitchen, why not set up the cheese center in the kitchen, the wine table in the dining room?

Besides the cheese, on trays, you need knives: a sharp-bladed knife to cut the firm cheeses, a butter knife or two for the softer ones. For an Edam or Gouda, a melon-ball cutter makes a fine scoop. Other than this, you need only paper napkins and small plates and an assortment of breads and crackers.

Besides French bread, you must have a selection of *bland* crackers. One to be especially recommended, though it is an expensive choice, is Bremner Wafers, manufactured by the Bremner Biscuit Company of Chicago. Another is the English import, Jacob's Cream Biscuits. The assortment of Jacob's Biscuits for Cheese is not bad, but the cream biscuits are better. Uneeda Biscuits now has an unsalted plain cracker; matzoh bread qualifies, and Norwegian flatbread is another possibility, though it is a bit crumbly when the cheese is so soft it must be spread on the wafers with a knife. Most American crackers are either too sweet, too salty, or contain too much shortening, though simple round crackers and saltines are not bad. Avoid any "barbecue-flavored" or cheese-flavored snacks if it's a tasting, though these may be put out for a big wine and cheese party. For any cheese tasting, sesame crackers are a good choice; they go nicely with both the soft bland and the more pungent cheeses and spreads.

If you are serving blue cheese, sweet butter should be put out, for many of these sharper blues taste far better if spread over a base of butter on French bread or pumpernickel—but make sure it's sweet, not the salted butter.

A wine tasting of three California red dinner wines, complemented by eight Danish cheeses. Starting with the red rind cheese, counterclockwise, they are Mini Fynbo, Samsoe, Tybo, Danish blue cheese, Danish Camembert, Danish Cream Cheese, Esrom and Havarti.

Bread sticks are good for nibbling between bites of cubed or sliced cheese, and thin-sliced salty rye is suitable for a party, where such cheeses as Swiss or caraway Cheddar are being offered.

If you feel you should offer something else besides cheese, fruit is the best idea, the kinds of fruit easiest to eat with fingers, such as bananas (very good with soft cheeses), grapes, crisp apples, black cherries, strawberries (with their caps on, so that they can be picked up and dipped into powdered sugar, or eaten plain). Or serve an assortment of vegetable relishes, such as celery, carrot, green pepper, and white turnip sticks. Black olives are excellent with mild-flavored cheeses, almost a must with feta and the chevret cheeses and very good with almost any cheese pâté spread. But avoid green olives with any wines except dry sherry, and also any kinds of pickles put up in vinegar, for the vinegar kills wine flavor. Toasted almonds and dry-roasted mixed nuts are suitable. If it's an offering of dessert wines or sparkling wines, you may offer macaroons or other simple crisp cookies. Recipes for these and for hors d'oeuvres made with cheese will be found in the final section.

It's wise to have plenty of flat coasters around, and if it's a party, not a tasting, ashtrays, too. There can be no doubt that smoking interferes with one's ability to taste wines critically, and those who do not smoke often feel inwardly annoyed when tobacco fumes fill the air. For a tasting, you might put up a "Please, No Smoking" sign at the entrance to the room where the wine tasting is to take place. But realistically, one must face the fact that those who are addicted to tobacco will not enjoy themselves if prevented from indulging in their habit. Therefore, it's essential to put ashtrays here and there—away from the tasting area, to avoid cigarette butts and ground-in ashes all over the place. And do be sure to have at least one window open, even in the dead of winter, unless you have a very effective air conditioner in operation.

Even when only a small amount is poured into each glass for tasting, some may not care about the sample and wish to empty the glass before trying another wine. Ideally, one should have a separate glass for each wine, but for practical purposes this is all but impossible. Therefore, it is suggested that a pitcher of water be kept on the wine table for the purpose of rinsing out the glass and a small ice bucket, porcelain pot, or casserole be kept handy where this rinse water can be emptied, as can wine samples tasters do not care for.

To clear the palate before going on to another wine, a bite of unbuttered bread is good. It removes the taste of the previous wine even better than water.

But the host must remember to keep the tasting samples small. After the tasting is finished, those who wish to go back for seconds to the wines they liked best should be encouraged to do so.

THE QUESTION OF WINE TEMPERATURE

It has always been an accepted rule that red wine should be served at room temperature, while white wine should be chilled, but from California the word has been proclaimed that the red wine should be served at cool room temperature, about 65 degrees Fahrenheit, and this has led many people to chilling red wines to cool them off. It is possible that in time the energy crunch will force many people to reduce their thermostats to 68 degrees, which is close enough, but even if room temperature remains at the more normal 72 degrees, chilling a red wine in the refrigerator is a dubious practice.

If the wine can be stored in a cooler place, in a wine cellar or room where the heat is shut off, fine. But the temperature should not be lower than 55 degrees, never under 40 degrees, as in a refrigerator. And if the wine is a full-bodied vintage wine, it needs to be opened at normal room temperature to "breathe" and to release the bouquet that is so important a test of a wine's quality. I've even known people to deliberately put uncorked bottles of red wine in a warm place to hasten this transformation of the wine. But this practice, too, is a dubious one.

Fruits and nuts surround this unusual three-tier cheese dish. The cheese could be served either as hors-d'oeuvres with a tasting of dry wines or with dessert wine, such as port, cream sherry, Madeira, Sauternes or other sweet wines.

From my many years of serving and enjoying red wines, it seems to me best that all red wine be served at room temperature, no matter how warm the room. And certainly for a tasting, there is no reason in the world to chill any of the red wines.

I have found that some of the softer, younger California red wines do take to slight chilling—the jug wines, especially, and the pasteurized wines. But these are wines that will not have an appreciable bouquet in any case, and if they are at all on the sweet side, chilling will help to mask that sweetness. All rosé wines need to be chilled; so should white wines, with the exception, as noted earlier, that vintage white wines with great bouquet can be better appreciated if not chilled.

The important thing is that none of the wines should be subjected to great and sudden changes of temperature. And if you are having a wine tasting in your home, the solution may be to reduce the thermostat purposely. People themselves raise a room's temperature; if you are having a crowd, a room with the thermostat set at 65 degrees will soon become quite comfortable.

One more thought: Wines offered for tasting in the tasting rooms of the California wineries are never chilled, any of them, with the single exception of champagne. All others are served at room temperature.

ADDING "ATMOSPHERE"

There are some people who feel it isn't really a party unless the place is brightened up with gay decorations. Travel posters may fulfill this desire: ask for them at travel agencies or tourist offices, or you may find some in art galleries or gift shops. Especially appropriate would be scenes from regions or countries noted for producing wines and/or cheese. These include several of our own states (California, New York, Washington State, Wisconsin) as well as such Old World countries as France, Switzerland, Germany, Sweden, Denmark, Norway, Italy, Spain, Portugal, Hungary, and Greece. That's a broad enough scope to allow for many possibilities. And if the host wishes to dress up in costume, the folk dress of any of the countries named would be appropriate, especially if the wines or cheeses to be served owe their origin primarily to a particular country. Flags of the countries or states might also be draped over the walls, or miniature flags inserted in arrangements of fruit or flowers.

Much easier (and I feel more appropriate) is simply to invoke a feeling of graciousness with candlelight, whose glow will be caught and reflected in the crystal of the glassware and the jewellike color of the wine. Or if it's a patio or lawn tasting, the soft light of Japanese lanterns or of burning flares can contribute the same sort of atmosphere.

Cheese and wine tasting for an informal buffet. The three California wines include a Rosé, a white Riesling, and a Burgundy, augmented by at least four cheese varieties.

THE "PECKING ORDER"

Bland cheeses and dry white wines always come first, followed by semidry whites and dry to semidry rosé wines—and with both these, bland or delicate cheeses go best. After the rosés come the red wines, and with these the more pungent or assertive cheeses may be offered.

Such a progression is not always as easy as it sounds. Many of the rosé wines are on the sweet side, and their sweetness can spoil the palate for a crisply dry red wine. Therefore if white, rosé, and red wines are to be tasted, the selection of rosés should be limited to the drier types. And if a wider range of white and rosé wines is wanted, why not restrict the tasting to only whites and rosés, no reds?

It would be my idea to hold a tasting of red wines alone, without white or rosés, but when I have discussed this with others who have attended and given tastings, they all disagree with me. More variety is needed, they insist, to make the occasion interesting. So even when it is essentially a red wine tasting, there could be one or two white wines to start, but dry types, especially when the reds to follow will include some that are tart or acidic.

Again we come to the question of whether the occasion is a serious tasting or a party. If it's the latter, the host may simply put out a selection of wines, ranging all the way form aperitifs to table wines and even a sweet wine. The guests may then select whatever they wish.

But for a serious tasting, the host must give sober thought to offering a progression of wines that will not cancel one another out. The first must be a quite dry and light white wine; if semisweet or sweet wines are on the agenda, they must be followed by red wines that are full bodied but not too astringent.

And while sharper and more robust cheeses go with the more robust red wines, if a sweet wine comes last, then the final cheese should be a soft dessert type. Fortunately all these go equally well with red wines.

As certain of the pungent and sharp cheeses can be paired with fortified wines, especially medium dry sherries, Sercial-type Madeira, and tawny port, it might work well to serve such an aperitif wine first, followed by a robust red wine. Then the cheese assortment could include one or more blue cheeses, a Swiss-type firm cheese, and a soft goat cheese.

IDENTIFYING THE ENTRIES

Blind tastings are always fun, because sampling wine then becomes a game. Who can guess the identities of the mystery wines? How will the reaction of the tasters compare with the opinions of the experts?

For a truly blind tasting, the labels on the bottles must either be removed entirely or pasted over, then each bottle bears only a number for identity. The host, of course, has a list showing which numbers mean which wines, but he does not reveal their identity until the game is over. Then, after results are tallied, the participants may go back to drinking the wine or wines of their choice.

But some people like to know what they are drinking when they taste it, so another way to give a tasting is to print the information about each wine on a card, and place the cards in front of the bottles. Then tasters can go back to check the information about each wine as they sample them. This has the advantage of helping the tasters to acquire a more lasting impression, and to be able to spot the wines by label later in liquor stores.

Another helpful system is to type up in duplicate (or photocopy or mimeograph) a list of the wines and cheeses to be tasted, by number and name, with space beneath each entry in which the participants can write down their own personal reactions. These should be handed out to the guests when they first arrive.

Even with such a list, the printed cards to stand before each wine are important. Again, each wine must have an identifying number, and the card should tell its generic, varietal, and proprietary name (if all this information is available, and the wine *has* a proprietary or commercial name) and place of origin, both state and wine area, if American, and if European, the wine region, town or commune, and vineyard —if known. If the vintage year is given on the label, try to determine whether or not this was considered an exceptionally good vintage year for that particular wine. Such information is often hard to come by, since vintage charts report only on the more famous vineyards, and because it was an exceptional year for one wine region does not at all mean it was better than average for another. If you don't know and can't learn anything about the year of vintage, at least indicate whether this is a wine that ages well, and should have acquired age before being drunk, or whether it is best when young.

Price is also of interest. Everyone wants to know about good, inexpensive wines. Also, your guests will want to determine whether they can detect the difference between the less costly and more expensive wines. And certainly there is no point in pretending you have bought only the costliest wines. That would be not only absurd snobbism, it would be defeating the purpose of the tasting.

If the vintner has given descriptive information on the label (a practice now followed by many American wine makers), add this to the card *but in quotes*. The tasters will not necessarily agree. There might also be a notation as to which type of cheese or cheeses would go well with the wine.

Cheese labels are also important. On each should be given the name of the cheese, the family or classification to which it belongs, and any other pertinent or interesting information, such as its place of origin and whether it is a copy of an Old World cheese. Such cards should be attached to cocktail picks and inserted into the cheese.

Preparing such labels will require quite a bit of time and may involve considerable research. But if your guests really want to know, the labels in themselves will make the tasting worthwhile.

In addition to providing as much background information as possible on the card, you should have pencils and small note pads for the benefit of those tasters who may want to jot down additional notes for their own future reference—how they reacted to each wine and each cheese, which ones were their favorites.

HOW TO TASTE WINE

The ritual of wine tasting is not just a put-on; it helps one to appreciate the subtle differences between wines. One should first hold the glass beneath one's nose, then put the nostrils as far inside the glass as possible, breathe in deeply and appreciatively, with eyes closed (as in prayer), then take a very small sip and roll it around the tongue, back and forth. Then swallow, and brood about the aftertaste lingering in your mouth. You will be surprised to learn that a wine sometimes tastes different at the back than at the front of the mouth!

The next sip should be just as small and just as thoughtful. Maybe this time you will detect something about the wine you didn't notice at first. Then, before the wine is finished, go to the cheese table and look for a cheese recommended as right for the wine you are tasting. Taste the cheese in the same critical way, only a crumb of it in the mouth at first, followed by a sip of wine. Do you, too, feel that they

Goblets such as these are ideal for tasting wine, allowing the taster room to savor the bouquet, roll the wine gently around the sides of the glass, and to appreciate the clarity by holding the glass up to the light by its stem.

"marry" well, or not? Don't be a rabbit. If you don't like the combination, say so. It's differences of opinion that make wine and cheese tastings fun.

The host should explain to any of the guests who have not done this kind of thing before how the wine should be sniffed, sipped, and rolled around the mouth, and why. And he/she must be the leader, one who encourages discussion and perhaps disagreement. The latter will help others to realize how personal wine reactions are.

CONTESTS, PRIZES, AND BACKGROUND MUSIC

Blind tastings offer the most provocative entertainment that can be devised. For a small group, guessing right is reward enough. But for a larger group, prizes should be offered to those who come up with the highest scores. Bottles of wine and packages of cheese, of course, make ideal prizes.

Wines chosen for a blind tasting should include several in each classification, and at least one imported wine to compare with American wines of the same name (generic or varietal). Each ballot will contain the name of the participant or voter, but there must be no verbal or whispered exchanges until all slips have been collected.

It is harder to conceal the identity of cheese than wine, because the shape of the package or the appearance of the cheese may give it away. Still, cheeses that are somewhat similar in appearance can be "blind tasted": blue cheeses, big-holed Swiss types, soft ripened cheeses of much the same size, shape, and color; or cheeses that are not sufficiently well known for the shape or appearance to give them away.

A more serious kind of contest is one that could only be presented to people who consider themselves already fairly knowledgeable. This, like school examinations, would consist of a written quiz containing true-or-false, multiple choice, and incomplete sentences. (A sample of such a quiz will be found on pages 133-135.) This would have to be mimeographed in advance and pencils provided the participants, then a "board of examiners," consisting of at least three persons, should be assigned to examine and grade the scores.

The examination could cover both wines and cheeses, or just one or the other, as desired. Since it requires considerable knowledge, it would be only fair to offer several prizes, a top prize for the highest scores, a first prize for those who did best with the wine questions, another prize for those who did best on questions about cheese, then second and third prizes for each of these categories, if the number taking part is large enough. This could be a good club project, one that would call for advance planning and the participation of a sizable number of people to share the cost of supplying prizes and the work of getting the examination ready.

What about background music for entertainment? Will it help or only be distracting?

For a party rather than a tasting, music, either live or stereo, is a great idea, if not too heavy. However, for serious tasting, entertainment is not needed, because the tasting in itself is provocation enough.

On the following pages, menus for both tastings and parties are suggested, for small groups and large (that is, up to forty persons; for larger gatherings than this, it may be better to make use of the services of a party consultant or caterer). Some menus concentrate on a particular class of wine, such as aperitif or dessert wines, in an attempt to cover the entire range of possibilities. Since it is more difficult to select the proper cheeses to serve with white or rosé wines, the wines in every case are suggested first, then the appropriate cheeses to serve with them.

Brand names are given purposely, for only in this way is it possible to learn how very different wines with the very same varietal or generic name can differ one from another.

In many cases, far more wines are suggested than you would want to offer, even if you could afford that luxury. This is because some of the wines mentioned are in quite limited distribution, or may be in adequate distribution in one part of the country but scarcely known in another area. The same is true of cheeses.

It is not necessary to serve anything but a selection of wine and a selection of cheese, plus breads and crackers to go with the cheese. However, I have been asked to include recipes for pâtés, cheese snacks, and other hors d'oeuvres or foods appropriate to serve at such occasions for the benefit of those who feel better if they can offer something they've made themselves. And also to please those who enjoy reading recipes whether they ever get around to making them up or not.

PARTY AND TASTING MENUS

INTIMATE EXPLORATORY TASTINGS

The best and most pleasant way to learn about both wines and cheeses is to have small, intimate tastings to which you invite friends you know want to increase their scope of gastronomic knowledge as much as you do. The best number to share such a tasting is between six and sixteen persons, no more.

Suppose you've dropped in at a wine and cheese shop, intending to pick up only a wedge of Brie and perhaps a bottle of red wine for dinner but, being obsessed by things gastronomic, you can't get away that easily. Before you leave, you've picked up five kinds of cheese and three wines you had heard about but not previously sampled. There's no other solution but to give a tasting!

Almost any time of day will do. After all, one doesn't taste wines with the intention of getting looped. Sunday brunch is fitting. And for such a gathering of friends, you needn't worry too much about whether the cheeses and the wines will "marry" properly. The very point is to find out by making comparative tastes, and letting each of your friends contribute an opinion.

This goes off so well, you determine next time to be more selective and deliberately choose wines that have something in common, for making comparisons.

For example, compare one of the better California Cabernets with a Bordeaux red, such as a Saint-Julien, or a Bordeaux wine bearing the varietal name Cabernet Merlot. Or pair an American wine called generically a Rhine wine (or a proprietary wine such as Gallo Rhinegarten) with a wine from the Rhineland of Germany, either one from the

Rheingau or a less expensive blended wine such as Zeller Schwarze Katz. Make similar comparisons with American wines: taste any jug wine called "chablis" with a Louis Martini or Weibel Pinot Chardonnay.

The first few times may be hit-and-miss combinations, but before long you will be putting much more thought into the selection, and coming up with a conversation-making assortment. And before you know it, you may have established your own little circle or club, the members of which will in turn hold tastings in their homes.

This kind of tasting is the only way to learn to appreciate the difference between wines, and to become thoroughly conversant with the best names in the wine business and the most subtle of cheeses.

Comparing wines differing greatly in price is another fascinating study. This makes for a good blind taste offering.

For example, remove the labels and offer Gallo Hearty Burgundy, widely proclaimed to be the best American wine for the price on the market (though, unfortunately, all that publicity has in many cases caused proprietors to up the price tag), alongside a red Rioja from Spain costing about $1.50, or a Chilean burgundy. For the same tasting, offer Sebastiani Barbera and Robert Mondavi Pinot Noir.

If serving nothing but red wines is dull, you might start out with two white, say Almadén Mountain White and Wente Brothers Le Blanc de Blancs, both American wines but the second costing considerably more than the first. Or, compare a Chenin Blanc such as Oakville's with Vouvray, a French white wine from the Loire valley made with the same varietal grape.

For the cheese on such an occasion, first offer Brie or a Camembert and Chantal with the white wine as a delicious beginning, to be followed by reds with a Sugarbush Stiltonbleu.

On another occasion, you may want to make a blind tasting of several soft ripened cheeses. Remove the labels from two Camemberts, one French, one American, to see who if any of those present can detect the difference and correctly identify them. Then do the same with a fontina from Sweden and a fontinella from Wisconsin, asking the contestants to guess which is an American cheese, which made in Europe, and in which country. Jarlsberg and a Swiss cheese could be compared "blind"; so could Esrom (a Danish Port Salut type) and Liederkranz.

For a formal tasting, you would never select cheeses so much alike, but for those serious about educating themselves, this is the only way to do it, and with an intimate group, perhaps only family and the couple next door, opinions can be expressed without restraint.

A friend who has frequently given such small informal wine tastings tells me that he always deliberately includes in each "blind tasting" at least one very poor wine, another that is inexpensive but reasonably good, and a premium wine that has been highly praised by experts. It is fascinating, he reports, to note the reaction on the faces of those who taste the poor wine, and equally interesting to observe that, more times than not, even the novices, those who know little about wine, "nearly always come to the same conclusions as the experts." They end by being convinced that the more expensive wines, in most cases, are well worth the difference in price.

But it doesn't always turn out this way. Sometimes lesser wines are chosen in preference to the expensive ones, and even wines rated by experts as being inferior may come out with a good "blind taste" score. Here is where individual preference enters in.

When the group is small enough, the tasting can be followed by a pot-luck dinner, with more of the same wine to go with the food.

On such an evening, you might try testing three wines called Cabernet Sauvignon, each from a different country: one from California, another from Chile or Yugoslavia, and a Saint-Emilion or petit château wine from Bordeaux, the region where the Cabernet Sauvignon grapes originated. With these, have Pipo Crem (a creamy blue cheese from Bresse), Havarti, and a well-aged Vermont white Cheddar cut from a wheel. A casserole, such as beef Bourguignon or a Hungarian goulash, could be waiting in the oven, and a salad, ready to toss, in the refrigerator.

Or some other evening start off with an American white wine, perhaps a varietal like Green Hungarian or a dry Chenin Blanc, and a Chilean Riesling. If you prefer to compare two quite different American white wines, the selection could be Christian Brothers Pineau de la Loire and Wine Makers Guild Rhineskeller.

Follow this with three quite different reds. Italian Swiss Colony Zinfandel, Inglenook Navelle Claret, and an Italian Piedmont wine such as Bardolino, or a Spanish red wine such as Federico Paternina 1964.

With the white wines, offer provolone cheese and Havarti, a Danish import available in many supermarkets. With the reds, Black Diamond Canadian Cheddar and one of the French goat cheeses would make good choices.

An evening like this might be a good time to test the difference between a red wine served immediately after uncorking and one uncorked at least an hour beforehand. But for such a test, select wines in the premium class and of vintages going back at least three or four years. For example, both might be Pinot Noir of a 1970 or 1971 vintage; or one might be a California Pinot Noir, the other a French wine, such as a Saint-Emilion.

It would be astonishing if all the wines and cheeses suggested above were locally available, especially in the same shop. Not only is it your privilege to make substitutions in this and the following menus, in most cases it probably will be necessary to do so. But by suggesting wines and cheeses not only by type but with the name of the winery or place of origin, it is hoped the exploring gourmet will have a better idea of what to look for and be inspired to become better acquainted with the products of outstanding vintners and cheese makers.

OPEN HOUSE FOR A MIXED GROUP (30 TO 40 PERSONS)

You want to throw a fun party for people who are acquaintances rather than friends, perhaps members of an organization to which you belong, or neighbors in a community in which you are a comparative newcomer. You don't know that much about their drinking habits or tastes, and feel reasonably sure that few of them are serious connoisseurs. There may be some among them who don't drink at all, not even wine. But being knowledgeable about wine and cheese, you can select combinations that will please all tastes.

For example, choose wines that are popular if not gourmet selections and offer them either straight (that is, in wine glasses), or on the rocks, or turn them into tall drinks by adding soda or orange juice, according to individual requests. For this you need someone to serve as bartender, but the drink recipes couldn't be more simple.

On another table you will have a selection of cheeses, but even if you have as many as forty guests, you need not have more than five different kinds of cheeses, plus perhaps two cheese spreads or pâtés. In fact, with so many people, you almost have to limit the selection, or there will not be enough of some of the smaller cheeses to go around.

Besides cheese, offer a variety of crackers, as well as relishes, black olives, and nuts.

Wines

Paul Masson Emerald Dry
Gallo Pink Chablis or Vin Rosé
Taylor Sangría

Christian Brothers Dry Amontillado Sherry

Wine Drinks

White or Pink Spritzer with Strawberries *(see below)*
Sangría with Fruit and Soda *(see below)*

Andaluz Cup *(see below)*

Cheeses

Jane's Pâté Ball *(see below)*
Cheddar in Sherry Spread *(see below)*

Jarlsberg
Fontinella
American Muenster

Accompaniments

Dry-roasted mixed nuts
Sesame crackers
Matzoh bread or Uneeda Biscuits (unsalted)
Bread sticks

Thin-sliced pumpernickel
Celery, black olives, carrot sticks, green pepper slivers

Pink Spritzer with Strawberries

For each serving, pour 3 ounces of either the white wine or pink chablis in a tall glass, then add ice cubes and soda to cover the ice. Stir well. Garnish each with half a strawberry.

Sangría with Fruit and Soda

For each serving, pour 2 to 3 ounces of bottled sangría over ice cubes in an old-fashioned glass, add about 1 tablespoon chopped canned peaches, a dash of the peach juice, a slice of lemon, and soda to fill the glass.

Having first learned about sangría in Spain, it has always astonished me that bottled sangría should be sold as a "wine." In Spain, this is a simple wine punch made of one-half part very ordinary red wine with usually one-fourth part lemonade, or a mixture of lemonade and other fruit, and one-fourth part club soda or sparkling water. Seasonal chopped fruit, almost any fruit in season, is added to the pitcher. Some people add a bit of brandy. But it is the simplest of punches-in-a-pitcher.

I suppose the reason for the popularity of the bottled sangría is that this is still easier to serve than having to prepare lemonade separately, and many drink it just as it comes from the bottle. The fact that the bottled mixture is now being made by so many firms indicates that it has universal popularity.

For a less expensive drink, I urge that you try making your own. Any red wine will do, though the cheapest of Spanish Rioja wines are preferable. Add a little juice from canned peaches, 1 peach chopped fine, lemonade made with frozen concentrate, and club soda. Repeats can be put together as easily as the first pitcherful. In season, the fresh peaches are even better.

A similar drink may be made with white wine, peaches, orange juice, and soda. Both are excellent summertime thirst quenchers.

Andaluz Cup

For each serving, place ice in an old-fashioned glass, add sherry to half fill the glass, then add orange juice in any proportion desired. Some like it mostly sherry with a little juice; others prefer it the other way round.

Jane's Pâté Ball

2 eight-ounce packages cream or farmer cheese, softened
1 five ounce jar Old English Cheese Spread
1 two-ounce wedge blue cheese
1 small onion, grated, juice and all
1 tablespoon Worcestershire sauce (optional)
1 cup finely chopped pecans
¼ cup minced parsley

When the cream or farmer cheese is soft enough to spread easily, combine with all the other ingredients except the nuts and parsley and form, using the back of a spoon, into a ball or inverted half-melon shape. Combine nuts and parsley and sprinkle mixture evenly over the surface of the cheese ball, pressing in lightly with the back of a spoon. Refrigerate, lightly covered with foil, for 24 hours. *Makes enough for 20 to 25 appetizer servings.*

Cheddar in Sherry

1 pound mild semifirm Cheddar, shredded
½ to ⅔ cup sherry

Soak the cheese in ½ cup sherry overnight, then whir in the blender until smooth, adding more sherry if a softer spread is desired. Serve from a shallow bowl, to be spread over sesame crackers or Melba rounds. *Makes 3 to 3½ cups.*

How much to buy? If you are expecting forty guests, allowing a half bottle or twelve ounces per person, you will need a total of four gallon-sized jugs or twenty twenty-four ounce bottles (fifths). This might be one gallon each of the Emerald Dry and Pink Chablis, two gallons of the sangría, and one gallon of dry sherry. Add six or eight quart-sized bottles of club soda, two six-ounce cans of frozen orange juice (reconstituted as needed), and the fruit cut up ready to add as garnish.

For the cheese, besides the cheeses needed for the pâté ball and Cheddar spread, you should buy approximately seven to seven and one-half pounds, which might consist of two pounds each fontinella and Jarlsberg and three to three and one-half of Muenster. It's best to buy these from a delicatessen or cheese specialty shop.

AN APERITIF TASTING FOR TWENTY

Instead of cocktails, a selection of aperitif wines may serve as the basis for a tasting for a somewhat more sophisticated group. But like the wine offerings at the open house, these may be offered plain, on the rocks, or in mixed wine drinks, as the guests prefer.

Wines
Pedro Domecq La Ina Sherry
Weibel Dry Bin or Cocktail Sherry
White Dubonnet
Rainwater Madeira or Leacock's Sercial

Paul Masson Double Dry Vermouth
Stock Sweet Vermouth
Cassis

Wine Drinks
Perfect Cocktail *(see below)*

Vermouth Cassis *(see below)*

Cheeses
Camembert
Cheshire

Bolina or Flora Blue Cheese (Danish)
Port Salut

Crackers and Bread
Pumpernickel, thinly sliced

Assorted crackers

Other hors d'oeuvres
Welsh Rarebit Dip *(see below)*
Baby gherkin pickles

Marinated green olives *(see Page 97)*

About the wines: La Ina is one of the most popular of all the imported dry sherries and is available almost everywhere. It is not the driest of the sherries—Tio Pepe has that honor—but it is preferred by most Americans to Tio Pepe. For comparison, it would be interesting to serve one of the California sherries made with the submerged flor by the solera method. If Weibel's Dry Bin is not to be found (in the East it is in very small distribution), try another domestic sherry labeled either "pale dry" or "cocktail sherry."

Rainwater Madeira in its characteristic straw-covered bottle is a superb wine, a Sercial type, which means it is one of the driest of the Madeiras.

Of the dry vermouths, unquestionably the finest is Noilly-Prat, the original "French vermouth." Many of the American vermouths labeled dry are actually quite sweet. The Paul Masson Double Dry is less sweet than others.

Sweet vermouths vary even more than the dry. Martini and Rossi is considered by many to be the best of the imported Italian vermouths, with a well-balanced flavor blend of herbs and spices. Others prefer Cinzano. Of the American sweet vermouths, I have suggested Stock because it seems less overwhelmingly sweet to me than some of the others and has a nice cinnamon spiciness to it. But selecting vermouths is even more a matter of personal taste than selecting table wines. And there are dozens to choose from.

In addition to Dubonnet (white or red), another popular aperitif that might be offered is Campari, an Italian import. This is very bitter, and should be served with club soda and a squeeze of lemon.

Cassis is rarely drunk by itself. A concentrated essence made from blackberries, it is most often served as a mixed drink with dry vermouth, a very popular aperitif with the French boulevardiers.

About the cheeses: Camembert may be served plain, but for an interesting appetizer you might try serving it the German way. For each person, place, on a bread and butter plate, half a wedge of the cheese and a small mound of minced fresh onion, butter, and a slice of pumpernickel. First the butter, then the cheese is spread on the bread, onion sprinkled over the cheese, and for those who want it, the pepper grinder is passed for a sprinkling of black pepper. Since this requires plates and butter spreaders for each person, you may find it easier to mix the ingredients and serve it as a pâté (see below).

Cheshire is a rather mild English cheese of the Cheddar family with a hint of smokiness in its taste, delicious both as an aperitif cheese and when served with white wine. If not available, brick or Muenster could be served instead.

Bolina is a new blue cheese from Denmark, creamy and not quite so assertive as the cheese usually called "Danish blue." Flora is the brand name of a particularly creamy blue from Denmark. Port Saluts vary from being very pungent to only moderately so. If possible, taste a sliver before purchase.

Marinated Green Olives

Pour off all or most of the brine from a jar of pimiento-stuffed green olives and cover with dry vermouth. Recap, marinate for several hours; drain before serving. The olives have a more delicate flavor, go better with wine than those with the saltier brine flavor.

Perfect Cocktail

The usual proportions are half sweet, half dry vermouth, but this can be varied according to taste. Combine in a cocktail shaker or a pitcher, blend well, and serve on the rocks with either a twist of lemon peel or a thin slice of orange. (Many like an orange slice and a dash of bitters with plain sweet vermouth on the rocks, while the dry vermouth drinkers may want a pitted cocktail olive or a lemon sliver in theirs.)

Vermouth Cassis

For each serving, pour dry vermouth over ice cubes in an old-fashioned glass, add a dash of cassis, enough to color the vermouth a pale pink.

(If cassis is not available, use either grenadine syrup in its place or combine dry vermouth with rosé wine, in proportions of 2 to 1, or half and half, adding a dash of grenadine syrup.)

Peppered Camembert

1 six-ounce box Camembert
¼ cup minced onion
Freshly ground black pepper to taste

An American Camembert will do for this, or second best, a Danish or German Camembert. It should be a firmer, blander cheese than the original French from Camembert. Scrape off the white crust, put in a blender with the onion and freshly ground black pepper and blend until smooth, about 30 seconds. Serve in a small bowl surrounded with pumpernickel slices; baby gherkins go well with it, too. *Makes enough for about 15 to 18 appetizer servings.*

Welsh Rarebit Dip

4 cups (1 pound) shredded sharp Cheddar cheese
½ cup milk
1 teaspoon dry mustard
Salt and freshly ground pepper to taste
2 tablespoons butter
1 egg, well beaten
Cubes of tart apple or honeydew melon

Combine the cheese, milk and seasonings in a chafing dish over hot water or in a fondue pot and heat, stirring occasionally, until the cheese begins to melt. Stir in the butter. Add a tablespoon or two of the melted cheese mixture to the beaten egg and blend well, then stir the mixture into the remaining cheese. Keep the cheese dip warm over hot water or, if it is in a fondue pot, over a flame; have small cubes of fruit and fondue forks handy, so guests can dip and twirl the fruit in the melted cheese, as for fondue. *Makes enough as an appetizer for 15 to 20 guests.*

How much to buy? When serving fortified wines, allow one-quarter to one-third bottle per person, for generally less of these is consumed than table wines. This means the seven wines suggested should be enough for twenty persons.

It is not necessary to have such a wide selection. You might have two kinds of sherry, one Spanish and one American, either the Dubonnet or Madeira but not both, and two bottles each of sweet and dry vermouth.

Of the cheeses, to serve twenty persons, one pound of each would be about right, that is, five pounds altogether (including the Cheddar for the Welsh Rarebit). Or you may want to buy only two four-ounce packages of Camembert and more of the others. Except for the blended cheeses, it is best not to cut or slice the others in advance, but allow the guests to serve themselves.

A WINE AND CHEESE BRUNCH FOR EIGHT

White wines make a great eye-opener on Sunday morning, something like a champagne breakfast, but actually many prefer a fine still white wine to champagne.

For variety, add a rosé wine, or perhaps two for comparative tasting. Three white wines and one rosé should be enough to serve eight persons for brunch, but the extra rosé might well be wanted if the brunch lasts into the afternoon. Or, instead of two rosé wines, you might want to finish up with a sweet wine, a Hungarian Tokaj or an oloroso sherry.

Wines

Casal Garcia Vinho Verde (Portuguese)

Louis Martini Johannisberg Riesling

Bolla Soave (Italian) or Robert Mondavi Blanc Fumé

Inglenook Napa Rosé

Concannon Zinfandel Rosé

Cheeses

Brie

Gourmandise

Cantal (French) or Samso (Danish)

Caciocavallo (Italian) or kashkaval (Bulgarian or Hungarian)

Bread

Sourdough, lightly toasted

Sit-down Menu

Strawberries in Orange Juice *(see below)*

Oeufs au Plat au Fromage *(see below)*

Mahogany Sausages *(see below)*

Hot Muffins or Rolls

Assorted jams and jellies

Coffee

About the wines: These are suggested as a progression from very dry and light to more full bodied. The driest white is Vinho Verde. This, however, may be hard to locate, so in its place you might serve Chilean Riesling or Sipon, a Yugoslav white.

The Louis Martini Johannisberg Riesling is a particularly fine sample of this varietal—delightfully dry, well balanced, and with lovely bouquet. Just a trace less dry is Soave, from the Italian Piedmont, a white wine that everyone likes. If the Concannon Zinfandel Rosé can be located, do include it. This is light, soft, drier and deeper in color than most rosés, and almost like a light red wine.

For the finale, after brunch is finished, a Hungarian Tokaj would make an exciting climax. Or introduce your friends to a very smooth, medium-sweet oloroso from Spain, Pedro Domecq Double Century.

About the cheeses: While the wines are being chilled, the cheeses must all be warmed to room temperature. Even better, remove them all from the refrigerator the night before. With the cheese, instead of crackers, have lightly toasted sourdough bread.

Strawberries in Orange Juice

Slice strawberries in half, dust with sugar, and cover with orange juice. Freshly squeezed orange juice is preferable but the frozen may be used. The strawberries taste surprisingly different when marinated this way.

Oeufs au Plat au Fromage

For this you need individual ramekins for each person. These come in two sizes, the smaller holding only one egg, the larger holding two. Whichever size is used, start by putting a small lump of butter, about a teaspoon, in each ramekin, and melt it in a preheated (400 degrees) oven. Then place a thin slice of provolone in each ramekin and add the egg or eggs. (For safety, break each egg first into a cup, and if the yolk does not break, then slip it into the ramekin. Do not use any with broken yolks.) Sprinkle salt over the eggs and dribble with about a teaspoon of whole milk or light cream.

If the ramekins hold only 1 egg each, place in the preheated oven for 5 minutes before serving. Ramekins holding two eggs require 10 minutes. Remove from the oven as soon as the whites are white throughout (no longer transparent), but while the yolks are still soft; make sure you have a potholder in each hand when you take the dishes from the oven. Serve sizzling at table, and eat with spoons.

Mahogany Sausages

2 nine-ounce cans Vienna sausages, drained, or 1 pound brown-and-serve sausages
¼ cup dry sherry
2 tablespoons soy sauce
¼ cup tomato catsup

Place the sausages in chafing dish with all the other ingredients. (If using brown-and-serve sausages, brown them first, then drain well on absorbent paper.) Heat until the sauce bubbles, then keep hot over hot water or a candle warmer. Serve with the eggs. *Makes 8 servings.*

AN EASY-DOES-IT TASTING AND DINNER FOR SIX

While half a bottle per person is normally considered enough for tasting, when guests are invited to remain for dinner, more wine should be allowed. For six people, four bottles of wine is not too much. In fact, better have a fifth bottle on hand.

Wines

Louis Martini Mountain Chablis   Sebastiani Barbera
Simi Fumé Blanc   Côtes du Rhône
Brolio Chianti Classico

Cheeses

Montrachet or another chevret   Stilton

Chiberta   Vermont white Cheddar

Dinner Menu

Baked Spaghetti-Ham-Lima Cas-   Toasted garlic bread
   serole *(see below)*   Flan Custards *(see below)*
Tossed salad with Stilton dressing   Coffee

About the wines: The wines are suggested in the order to be served, the chablis first; then the Fumé Blanc, which is a heavier semidry white; then Chianti, which is somewhat astringent; and finally a robust or heavy red wine. Barbera is a robust red wine, but the French Côtes du Rhône, from the same region as Châteauneuf-du-Pape, if well-aged, should have much the same "chewiness" and body.

About the cheeses: These are all gourmet cheeses, and should be fully appreciated by your more discriminating friends. Serve the Montrachet and Chiberta with the white wines, the others with the red wines. You need more cheese proportionately for a smaller group than a large: buy half a pound each of the Stilton and Cheddar (they will keep if left over), plus the roll of Montrachet (it comes in a package), and a wedge of Chiberta of about one-third pound.

About the dinner menus: The casserole can be prepared ahead, ready for the oven; then the oven need only be turned on while the wine tasting is in progress.

A salad dressing can also be prepared in advance, stealing a little from the Stilton for an oil and vinegar dressing. Either make it mixed greens (Boston lettuce, watercress, romaine, fresh spinach) or a combination cucumber-tomato-green pepper salad with chunks of feta cheese, if you happen to have any on hand. The salad can be prepared, except for the dressing, several hours beforehand and kept in the refrigerator, covered with stretchable plastic, until time to serve.

The custards can be baked the day before, chilled, then turned out onto plates in the hour before the tasters are due.

The garlic bread can be prepared ahead of time and then, wrapped *loosely* in foil so it will toast and the crust become crisp, placed in the oven during the casserole's last 15 minutes of baking.

Spaghetti-Ham-Lima Casserole for Six

   1 pound spaghetti, cooked and drained
   1 pound center-slice ham, cut into 1-inch-square pieces
   1 ten-ounce package frozen Fordhook lima beans
   2 cups spaghetti sauce of your choice
   ½ cup red wine
   Freshly grated Cheddar and Romano, or Swiss and Parmesan, mixed

In a well-greased long, shallow casserole, layer the spaghetti with the ham pieces, the lima beans, and the spaghetti sauce mixed with the red wine. Repeat until all the ingredients are used up, ending with the sauce, then spread a thick blanket of either of the grated cheese combinations on top.

Cover the casserole loosely with foil and bake at 375 degrees for 45 minutes, then lower the heat to 325 degrees, and continue baking for 15 minutes longer.

Flan Custards

2 cups milk
½ cup granulated sugar
2 teaspoons vanilla extract
3 eggs

You will need six individual Pyrex or metal custard cups or molds.

Heat together the milk, ¼ cup of the sugar, and 1 teaspoon of the vanilla; stir to be sure the sugar is melted. Beat the eggs until all-yellow but not foamy, then stir the warm milk into the eggs. Add the remaining vanilla. Place the remaining sugar in a small heavy pan or skillet over moderate heat, just until the sugar is completely liquified and golden. Spoon a little more than 1½ teaspoons of the syrup into the bottom of each custard cup or mold, swirling it up on the sides, then add the egg-milk mixture in equal portions. Place the cups or molds in baking pan, add water to ½ inch. Bake in a preheated 400-degree oven until the tops are lightly browned and a knife inserted in the center will come out clean, about 30 minutes. Remove from the oven and cool to room temperature, then chill thoroughly.

To remove from the cups, run a sharp knife around the edge, invert on a plate, then shake (holding the cup or mold with one hand, the plate with the other), until the custard comes out, which should be immediately. If not, run the knife around the edges once more and give another shake. A delicious, easy dessert.

Note: Sherry or brandy can be substituted for the second teaspoon of vanilla.

A LAWN TASTING

The popularity of rosé wines with Americans has led to the development of an extraordinary range of wines with delicate to deep rose color, from tart to sweet. Since chilled rosés are especially liked in summer, this suggests a good kind of tasting to hold on the lawn. Two extension tables can be set up, one for the wines, the other for the cheeses, and in case of unexpected showers, an open-sided tent can be put up to serve as a pavilion.

With the rosé wines, offer two whites for variety, a selection including both American and imported samples. The French were the first to introduce rosé, and have some especially fine ones. The best are from the Loire Valley and Provence, the Côtes du Rhône region.

Allowing half a bottle per person, select, from among the following, whichever ones you are able to find in your favorite shop. Serve in the order given, from the driest to the semisweet.

White Wines

Sterling Vineyards Pinot Chardonnay

White Rioja (Age, Primavera, Federico Paternina)

Wine Masters Guild Vino de Tavola White

Pouilly-Fumé (Loire)

Château Wente or Sweet Sauvignon Blanc

Rosé Wines

Mirassou Petit Rosé

Santa Comba or Mount Estoril

Tavel Rosé (French)
Almadén Grenache Rosé
Widmer Pink or Boordy Rosé
(New York)

Rosé (Portuguese)
Oakville Gamay Rosé
Hudson Valley or Mogen David
Pink Catawba

Cheeses
Feta with black olives
Grappo or crème de Gruyère
Caerphilly

Bondost
Swiss or Blarney

Other Hors d'Oeuvres
Blooming Hors d'Oeuvres Bush   Cheese Sticks
(see below)

About the wines: Even if this is a mixed group, it's worth serving two or three outstanding (and more expensive) wines for comparison with lesser ones. The Sterling Pinot Chardonnay, for example, is a beautiful example of a crisp, light, well-balanced white wine. If your favorite liquor store does not have Sterling, try a Chardonnay from one of the other small but renowned California wineries.

If you can find an Age white Rioja, you will be surprised how good it is for the price, and it should be judged on this basis. The Wine Tasters Guild wine is suggested for comparison's sake. Many wineries now produce what they call "mountain wines," which do not pretend to be as good as the varietals but should be of a better quality than other generic wines, and you might prefer to offer one of these.

Pouilly-Fumé is a semidry white from the Loire Valley of France. If not available, perhaps you could find a Muscadet from the same wine region.

Château Wente is a dessert wine, not a table wine, and should really be offered after the rosés. Sweet Sauvignon Blanc is also a dessert wine, but made primarily with Sauvignon Blanc grapes, while the Château Wente uses primarily Sémillon. This is the American counterpart of a French Sauternes. (And to show the difference between what is meant by Sauternes in France, and the American white wines called sauterne, you might add to this list any generic white sauterne.)

Half a dozen different rosé or pink wines are suggested to show what a wide range of wines are now produced in this category. The Mirassou Petit Rosé is the driest of them all, made with Petite Sirah grapes, the same used in making the heavy red wines of the Rhône valley in France. It has become so popular in California that it represents 15 percent of all wine sales at Mirassou. Tavel is the finest of the French rosés, made with the Grenache grape. To compare this with Almadén Grenache Rosé would be interesting, because Almadén was the first to introduce this rosé varietal to the United States, in an attempt to make a wine like Tavel.

Because the Portuguese rosé wines have become so popular, at least one should be added to the tasting, and the two brands named are less expensive but of approximately the same quality as the better-known Mateus. Several California wineries now make rosé with the Gamay Beaujolais grape, and Oakville Gamay Rosé is a fine sample. In the East most rosé and pink wines are made with native American grapes, though the Boordy Rosé is from a French hybrid variety. The Pink Catawba is quite as sweet as the Sweet Sauvignon Blanc; the two might be served together, at the conclusion of the wine tasting.

About the cheeses: Delicate-flavored cheeses must be served with both white and rosé wines. All those suggested above will go well with both, though it is easier to mate white wines with a variety of cheeses than the rosés. Caerphilly, the Welsh cheese, is fine with rosé, and a mild Swiss type is also suitable. Blarney is the Irish version of the big-holed firm cheese family.

Blooming hors d'oeuvres bush: To make a colorful centerpiece for the hors d'oeuvres table, buy an inexpensive white styrofoam ice bucket and turn it upside down on a platter or tray. Insert various small nibbles, including a variety of cheese balls, into the styrofoam with toothpicks, so that it is almost entirely covered.

Suitable "flowers" for the bush would include cherry tomatoes, or better, tiny yellow plum tomatoes if these are in season; pitted California black olives; pineapple chunks, fresh or canned; and cheese balls in several colors. Recipes for cheese balls follow.

Parsleyed Cheese Balls

> 1 eight-ounce package cream or farmer cheese, softened
> 3 to 4 tablespoons milk
> ¼ cup grated Cheddar
> Dash salt
> ¼ teaspoon crushed cumin (optional)
> 1 cup minced fresh parsley

Blend together all the ingredients except the parsley, using the lesser amount of milk if you are using farmer cheese. Shape into 1-inch balls and chill until firm. Roll in the parsley until well coated on all sides, then chill again until time to place on the "bush." *Makes about 25.*

Red Cheese Balls

Make the cheese balls as for Parsleyed Cheese Balls but roll half of them in paprika instead of parsley. Instead of cumin, the cheese may be spiced with powdered ginger or dry mustard. *Makes about 25.*

Nut-Crested Cheese Balls

Make the cheese balls in the same way as for Parsleyed Cheese Balls but roll them in coarsely crushed pecans, almonds, or walnuts. *Makes about 25.*

Sesame-Seeded Cheese Balls

> 2 cups (½ pound) shredded Swiss or brick cheese
> ¼ pound (1 stick)) butter or margarine, softened
> ½ cup sesame seeds, toasted until golden

Combine the cheese and butter and beat until very smooth, then shape into 1-inch balls and chill until firm. Roll the balls in the toasted seeds and chill again.

Note: If preferred, use mild Cheddar instead of Swiss and roll the balls in shelled, salted sunflower seeds instead of sesame. *Makes about 25.*

Cheese Sticks

½ package or 1 stick pie crust mix
½ cup shredded Swiss, Cheddar, or American cheese
½ cup minced walnuts

Prepare the pie crust according to package directions and roll out into square shape. Combine the cheese and nuts and cover the pastry with the mixture, then lay waxed paper over the top and press with a rolling pin. Cut into strips ½ by 2 inches. Freeze until an hour before serving time, then transfer to a baking sheet and bake in a preheated 450-degree oven until golden, about 6 minutes. *Makes about 18.*

Note: Double the ingredients to make 36 to 40.

A BRIDGE CLUB
TASTING AND LUNCHEON FOR EIGHT

Dreaming up something new, intriguing, and yet light to serve to one's fellow club members before settling down to the seriousness of an afternoon of bridge seems to be a common problem. A wine and cheese tasting could be an easy solution, with a casserole and salad for the sit-down lunch.

This is suggested as a luncheon menu, but if the club is meeting for an evening of bridge, it could just as well become a supper. (The menu is suitable for any "ladies' luncheon" or for any professional group meeting in a member's home.)

Wines

Blanc de Blancs de Leperon
 (French Pyrénées)
Gallo Sauvignon Blanc

Louis Martini Gamay Rosé or
 Rosé d'Anjou (Loire)
Almadén Grenoir Original

Cheese

Dofo Danish Brick
Coulommiers or Syrian braided
 cheese

Wensleydale
Shrimp Cheese Balls *(see below)*

Luncheon Menu

Chicken Divan *(see below)*
Hot Cheese Biscuits *(see below)*
Individual Tomato Aspics with
 Roquefort Dressing *(see below)*

Petits fours
Coffee or Tea

About the wines: Blanc de Blancs de Leperon is a crisply dry white wine from the Pyrenees, much like a white Graves. If not available, any of the French white "country wines" could be served instead. Sauvignon Blanc is one of the new "premium varietals" recently introduced by Gallo, described as "completely dry . . . flinty and flowery." Among other of these new premium varietals, Gallo has a dry Chenin Blanc and a Riesling.

Several of the California wineries now make a Gamay Rosé, so if a Louis Martini is not available, one of the others might be. Cresta Blanca also has a Gamay Rosé. Or look for the Simi Rosé Cabernet.

Almadén Grenoir Original is a light red wine made with the Grenache grape, the same as used in their famous Grenache Rosé. A somewhat similar choice would be the Paul Masson Rubion.

If a heavier red wine is preferred, Sebastiani Zinfandel or Concannon Petite-Sirah would be appropriate.

The white and rosé wines should be chilled, the red wines uncorked before serving.

About the cheese: The three cheeses suggested are all bland enough to go well with both white and rosé wine, and will be good with the red, too. Coulommiers is in the Camembert class. If Wensleydale is not available, you can't go wrong with a wedge of good Switzerland Swiss.

The shrimp cheese balls can be considered a low-calorie hors d'oeuvres, to be offered with the wine, for those worried about consuming so much cheese.

About the luncheon: Everything on the menu can be prepared ahead. The shrimp balls can be shaped, chilled, and refrigerated until time to serve. The casseroles can be put together, ready for the oven, the previous day and kept refrigerated until about an hour before placing in the oven. Start preheating the oven about the time the tasting begins.

The tomato aspics can also be prepared the day before and unmolded the morning before the luncheon. The dressing can be ready in a serving pitcher or small bowl.

Mix the biscuits, have them cut and ready on a baking sheet to pop into the hot oven during the last 10 minutes before the meal is to be served.

Petits fours are tiny individual cakes that can be purchased from a bakery. These are a good dessert choice, for if a number of people pass up the cakes, the remainder can be frozen to serve some other time.

Remember to warm up the cheeses (to room temperature) an hour, at least, before guests are due.

Chicken Divan

4 whole chicken breasts
Salt
3 ten-ounce packages frozen broccoli spears
2 ten-and-one-half-ounce cans condensed cream of chicken soup
½ cup cream
½ cup grated Swiss cheese
1 egg, beaten
¼ cup freshly grated Parmesan cheese

Simmer the chicken breasts in salted water until tender, about 25 minutes. Drain, saving the broth. Bone the breasts and slice the meat as neatly as you can, saving any scraps to add to the sauce. Set the meat aside.

Separate the broccoli spears and place in a saucepan. Add salt and *boiling* water to cover, bring again to a boil, and cook just 3 minutes, leaving the cover of the pan slightly ajar so steam will escape. (This will help to keep the spears bright green.) Drain and set aside.

Make a sauce by blending the cream of chicken soup with 1 cup of the reserved broth and the cream. (If there is less than 1 cup of broth, add water to make the difference.) Stir in the Swiss cheese and beaten egg and beat to blend.

Divide the partially cooked broccoli between two long, shallow 1½-quart casseroles. Cover with half the sauce, then add the chicken slices and cover with the remaining sauce. Sprinkle half the Parmesan cheese over the top of each casserole and refrigerate if desired. (If refrigerated, remove from the refrigerator at least 1 hour in advance.)

Preheat the oven to 350 degrees and bake the casseroles for 30 to 40 minutes, until the sauce is bubbling and the tops are lightly browned. Serve hot. *Each casserole makes 4 to 6 servings.*

Shrimp Cheese Balls

2 three-and-one-half-ounce jars Danish or Norwegian baby shrimp, drained
1 eight-ounce package farmer cheese, softened
⅛ teaspoon powdered ginger
⅛ teaspoon curry powder
¼ teaspoon paprika

If you have a blender, add the ingredients in the order given, with blender in motion. Otherwise, mash the drained shrimp in a deep narrow bowl and beat in the cheese a quarter at a time, finally beating in the seasonings. Chill about 1 hour, then form into 1-inch balls. Serve this way or rolled in minced parsley. *Makes about 15.*

Hot Cheese Biscuits

2 cups biscuit mix
½ cup grated Cheddar cheese
½ cup milk

Blend cheese with the biscuit mix, then stir in the milk to make a stiff dough. Roll out on a floured board, cut out rounds with a biscuit cutter, and place on a baking sheet. Set aside until 10 minutes before serving time, then bake in a preheated 450-degree oven.

Tomato Aspics with Roquefort Dressing

Use any favorite recipe for tomato aspic, but chill in individual salad molds. Early on the day of your luncheon, unmold over lettuce on salad plates. Keep chilled until time to serve. A commercial Roquefort dressing may be used, or make your own:

Roquefort Dressing

2 tablespoons crumbled blue cheese
¼ cup sour cream
½ cup mayonnaise

Blend together crumbled blue cheese, sour cream, and mayonnaise and beat until smooth. Then dribble a little dressing over each aspic and pass the rest. *Makes 1 cup dressing.*

YOUNG ADULT
WINE AND CHEESE PARTY FOR THIRTY

It is disturbing to learn that the number of teen-age alcoholics is on the increase, even more so when many of them apparently depend for their highs on drinking quantities of wine.

Yet there are other young people in their late teens and early twenties who are discriminating enough to enjoy wine as it should be enjoyed, not as a beverage to produce a high, but as one with subtlety and gentle charm, to be savored primarily for flavor and fragrance and not downed quickly for its effect.

By "young adults" we mean, of course, those who have reached legal drinking age. Perhaps one reason that alcoholism has spread among those younger than this is that they have been introduced to wine and other alcoholic beverages too soon, before they are mature enough to show judgment in their drinking habits.

All beginning wine drinkers tend to prefer the sweeter wines, one reason why Mateus Rosé became such an overnight favorite with young people the world around. It would be foolish at a party of this kind to buy costly premium wines, for few among those present are likely to appreciate such wines—not yet. But there should be interesting variety, enough to let them realize how much fun it is to learn to distinguish the difference between wines, even those with the same generic and varietal names.

This is the kind of party that should take place out of doors, weather permitting, or in a family room that has a bar from which the wine can be dispensed. Buy wine in gallons or half gallons, but for convenience in serving decant it into carafes or pitchers. Keep servings small, no matter what kind of glasses are used.

The young people, if taught the proper way to sniff and taste wine, rolling it around the mouth from front to back, may be intrigued into making a game of this. In any case, they should not simply down the wine like water—or beer.

Several different wines are suggested in each category, even though a total of four gallons should be sufficient. Serve at least two better-quality wines, in half gallons or magnums, in the hope that some of those present will note the difference.

Wines

Almadén Mountain White Chablis, or Weibel Classic Chablis
Gallo Rhinegarten
Taylor Vin Rosé
Mateus Rosé

Age Rioja Rosada
Italian Swiss Colony Zinfandel
Wine Growers Guild Vino de Tavola Red or Petri Burgundy

Cheese

Feta
Gourmandise
American Muenster
Old English or Cracker Barrel Sharp Cheddar

Sliced American and Swiss cheese (for sandwiches)

Supper Menu

Swiss Pizza *(see below)*
Make-your-own Sandwich Buffet
  (see below)

Fruit bowl
Assorted cookies
Coffee

About the wines: The wines suggested, all available in half gallons or gallons, offer a good cross-section. None are premium or vintage wines, yet most of them are sound wines and pleasant enough for adults to serve at a more sophisticated gathering.

But to encourage young people to launch out into trying the finer wines, you might also have a half gallon of a Louis Martini or Robert Mondavi wine for comparison with Wine Growers Guild wines or Petri. Italian Swiss Colony Zinfandel has been praised by many wine drinkers as a better than ordinary *vin ordinaire.*

By all means, be ready to mix up a sangría punch (see the recipe on page 94), using frozen lemonade concentrate as a shortcut, adding club soda and fresh fruit (or chopped canned peaches). This can be served after the tasting is over, for it is sweet enough and light enough in alcohol to be a pleasant late-evening drink, one to follow the buffet supper.

About the cheese: All the cheeses suggested are universally popular. Gourmandise is the most costly of the lot, so buy only a limited quantity and offer it in small servings. But it is bound to be adored.

Swiss Pizza

The easiest and probably the most satisfactory way to prepare pizzas is to order them from a local pizza parlor or spaghetti joint that caters especially to the young. Then you can order two or three variations, and tell the chef at what time you will pick them up, hot from the oven.

Actually, pizzas with a tomato sauce filling, or made with hot (spicy) sausages, should be served only with red wine, and preferably a rather astringent red wine.

The best pizza I ever tasted (though I readily admit I have never been a pizza freak) was in, of all places, Switzerland. The dough was more like bread dough, there was more cheese on top and much less tomato sauce for the filling. The following is an approximation of that pizza, as nearly as long-distance memory can reconstruct it.

Basic Pizza Dough

1 envelope active dry yeast
1 cup warm (not hot) water
1 teaspoon salt
2 teaspoons vegetable oil
3½ cups all-purpose flour
½ teaspoon granulated sugar

Swiss Topping

1 cup or 1 eight-ounce can spaghetti sauce
1 cup chopped ham

½ cup chopped, pitted black olives
1 three-ounce can sliced mushrooms, drained
3 cups shredded Swiss cheese
1 cup shredded Cheddar or American cheese
½ cup freshly grated Romano cheese

Prepare the dough first. Dissolve the yeast in the water. Stir in the salt and oil, then gradually add the flour and finally the sugar. Beat until smooth, then turn out onto a lightly floured board or counter and knead the dough until elastic. Place in deep, greased bowl; brush the top with additional oil, cover lightly, and let rise in a warm place until doubled in bulk. Punch the dough down, divide in half, and roll each half into a ball. Then, using your fingers, press the balls of dough to fit two oiled pizza pans (14 inches in diameter), but handle lightly and do not make the crust as thin as for regular pizzas. Let rise again until doubled in bulk.

When the dough is ready, put on the topping. Brush each piece of dough with half the tomato sauce, then sprinkle with the chopped ham and chopped black olives, the mushrooms, and then the mixed cheeses, dividing and distributing as evenly as possible. Bake in a preheated 450-degree oven for 20 to 25 minutes, or until the crust is golden. Cut while warm into 8 portions. *The two together make 16 servings.*

Note: You may want to supplement these with baked-to-order pizzas, picked up ready to serve.

Make-Your-Own Sandwich Buffet

Put the makings of sandwiches on a long table or kitchen counter, urging the young people to make their own in whatever combination they like. The following ingredients are suggested.

Breads
French bread, sliced lengthwise (for heroes)
Thin-sliced white sandwich bread
Sliced rye or pumpernickel

Fillings
Sliced salami and/or bologna
Thin-sliced ham
Sliced tomatoes
Sliced red onions
Pimiento cut in squares
Head lettuce
Sliced American and Swiss cheese

Sauces and Seasonings
Butter
Prepared mustard
Mayonnaise
Caesar salad dressing

Sweet relish
Hot dog relish

For the softer cheeses, have also a selection of crackers, and for nibbling, potato chips, corn chips, and bread sticks.

How much to buy? If it's a Friday or Saturday night party, expect the merrymaking to go on long past midnight, which means you need considerably more wine than for a wine tasting. But since a gallon is equivalent to five twenty-four-ounce bottles, and adding ice and soda to wine also helps make it go farther, for thirty young people, a total of four gallons—or four half gallons or magnums and two full gallons—should be ample. In fact, it's wise not to buy too much, for that could encourage too much hilarity.

For the cheese, allow a quarter-pound per person or a total of seven and a half pounds. The bulk of this could be the sliced sandwich cheese.

A SHERRY AND CHEESE TASTING

There is such an enormous range of taste, color, bouquet, and degree of sweetness among sherries that they deserve a tasting all of their own. I don't know whether anyone has ever tried lining up American sherries against the Spanish, but I think it should be done for a group already fairly knowledgeable about wine and eager to learn more.

While a few California wineries are now producing dry sherries that more closely resemble the Spanish finos, using a submerged flor yeast and the solera method of alternately aging and blending, for the most part, American dry or cocktail sherries bear very little resemblance to the Spanish finos. In a blind tasting, I'm willing to swear that certain of them could be mistaken for dry vermouth. (I once commented innocently, when served a "cocktail sherry," that this was quite a nice vermouth!) Few of these sherries are really dry—though the same charge can be leveled against some of the less expensive imported sherries with misleading "pale dry" labels.

The three main classifications of Spanish sherries are (1) fino, the driest; (2) amontillado, which begins as a fino but develops deeper color, a "nuttier" flavor, and greater bouquet; and (3) oloroso, the sweetest and most fragrant, with which the cream sherries are made. But within each of these classifications there are such ranges and such variety that some "dry" sherries are as sweet or sweeter than some of the amontillados or those labeled "medium dry."

Besides the sherry wines of Spain, very similar are manzanillas (even drier and more saline) and the montillas, which come from vineyards near the city of Córdoba.

It might be of interest to include in such a tasting at least one Madeira and a Marsala, to see how these wines compare with American wines called "sherry," and with the Paul Masson Madeira.

Both the four-ounce tulip-shaped sherry (or whiskey sour) glasses and old-fashioned glasses should be put out on the wine table, because after the first comparative tasting, a good many will want to continue additional samples of sherry on the rocks. Do urge that they try each straight the first time, however. The subtlety of sherry, any sherry, simply cannot be appreciated when watered down with ice. Dry sherries may be chilled before serving.

The following suggests American and imported sherries to pair together for comparison.

Very dry

Tio Pepe or Rivero Fino de Jerez (Spanish)

Almadén Flor Fino or Solera Dry Cocktail (American)

Semidry to semisweet

Williams & Humbert Dry Sack or Duff Gordon Amontillado (Spanish)

Paul Masson or Christian Brothers Amontillado (American)

Cream or Oloroso

Harvey's Bristol Cream (Spanish)

Taylor New York State Cream Sherry or Gallo Livingston Cream Sherry (American)

Cheeses

Brie
Natural Gruyère or Crème de Gruyère
Bonbel

Chutneyed Cream Cheese Canapés (see below)
Liptauer Cheese Cone (see below)

About the wines: The American dry sherries that most closely resemble the Spanish finos include, beside the Almadén Flor Fino, Paul Masson Rare Flor, Weibel Dry Bin, and Concannon Prelude. These have been slow to reach wine stores in the East because, I am told, there is notable lack of demand for them. If more people asked for them, they would be stocked.

Sherry, especially a dry sherry, makes the perfect before-dinner aperitif when wine is to be served with the meal. The medium-sweet sherries, which include amontillado, are also appropriate for before-dinner drinks, far better than cocktails if fine wines are to be served later.

About the cheese: It is almost as difficult to select a proper cheese for sherry as for rosé wines. Only the more delicate and bland cheeses marry well with the drier sherries and even with the sweeter sherries one must avoid strong-flavored cheeses. If Brie is offered, I strongly urge that it be purchased from a cheese specialty shop and that it be so soft as to be almost runny. Supermarket cheeses called Brie are not typical, probably because they have been stored in too cold a temperature and have lost their moist creaminess.

Chutneyed Cream Cheese Canapés

½ cup damson plum preserves
4 dried apricots, chopped fine

¼ cup dry sherry or white wine
½ teaspoon curry powder, or to taste
¼ teaspoon crushed ginger
⅛ teaspoon cayenne pepper
2 tablespoons vinegar, or more to taste
1 three-ounce package cream cheese or 3 ounces farmer cheese
Bremner or other bland crackers

Make a chutney by combining all ingredients except the cheese and crackers in a saucepan and simmering over low heat until well-blended, stirring constantly; do not permit the mixture to stick to bottom of pan. Pour into bowl. Cool to room temperature but do not chill. Spread the crackers with the cream cheese, spoon just a little chutney over the top of each, and arrange on a platter.

Note: The chutney, which makes about 1 cup, will keep for other uses. You can also make a pineapple chutney: use 4 pineapple chunks, chopped, or one-third cup well-drained crushed pineapple instead of the chopped dried apricots.

Liptauer Cheese Cone

1 eight-ounce package cream or farmer cheese, softened
2 tablespoons butter, softened
1 anchovy fillet, minced
1 teaspoon prepared mustard
1 teaspoon caraway seeds, crushed
½ teaspoon paprika
Capers for garnish

Combine all the ingredients except the capers and blend until smooth. Form into a tall cone with a spatula, then, with the back of small spoon, make indentations down the sides in a swirl. Press the capers in lines along the indentations and chill. Serve with thin-sliced pumpernickel or rye crispbread. *Makes 1 cup.*

Besides the cheeses, and appropriate bread and crackers to serve with them, offer toasted, salted almonds and green and black olives. Sherry is one of the few wines with which green olives go well.

How much to buy? For a tasting, six bottles should be ample for as many as eighteen persons, since a quarter bottle is about right for each person. On the other hand, what is left over will keep almost indefinitely, so it is wiser to buy extra.

A FONDUE PARTY
AND WINE TASTING FOR TWELVE

Fondue is a popular supper dish with everyone, and since white wine goes well with it, this is a good opportunity to have a white wine tasting. But you might serve a selection of red wines as well, so that your tasters can decide whether they prefer white or red wine to accompany fondue.

You might make the tasting a blind one for the white wines before the fondue is served, bringing out the red wines later.

Besides the fondue, it would be well to offer several nibbling cheeses while the fondue is bubbling. You might also serve cheese-stuffed celery sticks, radishes, black olives, and crisp carrot sticks as appetizers.

The following white wines are suggested as offering a range from quite dry to semisweet. Cover up labels, give them numbers, let guests guess which is which, naming their preferences, and write down ratings: "fair," "good," "great."

White Wines

Petri Chablis Blanc
Dr. Konstantin Frank Johannis-
  berg Riesling
Bully Hill Seyval Blanc

Hugel Gewürztraminer (Alsatian)
  or Neuchâtel (Swiss)
Adriatica Sipon (Yugoslav)

Red Wines

Inglenook Navalle Claret
Beaujolais-Villages (French)

Jouvet Coteaux de Tricastin

Nibbling Cheeses

Dofo Danish Brick
Brindza

Fontinella

Fondue Party Menu

Radishes, black olives,
  carrot sticks
Celery Stuffed with Nutted
  Cheese *(see below)*

Classic Cheese Fondue
  (see below)

About the wines: A wide selection of white wines is suggested, more than is needed for a group of twelve persons, but then it's unlikely that all these would be available in the same shop.

The Petri Chablis Blanc is suggested for contrast to the next two very fine American white wines. Dr. Frank's Johannisberg Riesling has received such extravagant praise as being the first European type varietal to thrive in upper New York State that it's worth knowing about. So is the Bully Hill Seyval Blanc. Be sure to purchase both several days in advance to give them a good rest, then chill for not more than half an hour and open another half hour before pouring. Serve them in big goblets so the bouquet can be fully appreciated.

Gewürztraminer or Neuchâtel are the wines that would be served with a fondue in Switzerland, and one of these should be the white wine to go into the mixture (see recipe below). The Yugoslav Sipon is a very pleasant, fruity wine.

Of the three reds suggested, the Navelle claret is not Inglenook's finest red wine, but is interesting as a red *vin ordinaire*. It is a light wine, and so, in one sense, in the same class as a French Beaujolais. The Coteaux de Tricastin, an inexpensive light red wine from southern France not far from the Bordeaux wine region, does not need uncorking in advance, yet has a full-bodied nose and an aftertaste that could almost be a young Burgundy.

About the cheese: The three cheeses suggested do not need crackers with them; all can be cut in chunks and eaten with the fingers. The Dofo Danish brick is a new and most delightful cheese, very good with white wines and equally right with reds.

Celery Stuffed with Nutted Cheese

1 three-ounce package cream cheese or ½ (eight-ounce) package
   farmer cheese, softened
⅓ cup shredded mild Cheddar
½ cup chopped or coarsely crushed dry-roasted peanuts
1 bunch Pascal celery, cut in 2-inch lengths

Combine the cream or farmer cheese, Cheddar, and nuts and blend
until well mixed. Use as a stuffing for celery, putting about 1 tablespoon of cheese in each 2-inch length. *Makes 1 cup cheese mixture.*

Classic Cheese Fondue

1 clove garlic
2 cups dry white wine
½ pound natural Gruyère, shredded (2 cups)
½ pound Swiss or Emmentaler, shredded (2 cups)
¼ pound sharp Cheddar, Appenzeller, or fontinella, shredded (1 cup)
1½ tablespoons all-purpose flour
3 tablespoons kirsch or brandy
Dash nutmeg or black pepper
French or sourdough bread, cut into 1-inch cubes

To make this, you must have a fondue casserole or any round shallow
casserole that can be used over an alcohol burner or electric fondue
unit. Or you can use a chafing dish.

Blend together the three cheeses and the flour and set aside. Crush
the garlic over the casserole to release the garlic juice, then discard
the garlic. Pour in the wine, heat until tiny bubbles appear, then toss a
handful of the cheese-flour mixture into the wine and stir. Add the
remaining cheese by handfuls, stirring until smooth after each. Keep
the heat low at all times. When all of the cheese has been added, stir
in the kirsch or brandy and sprinkle with nutmeg or pepper.

To eat, spear cubes of the bread on long-handled fondue forks and
twirl the bread with the melted cheese, trying to get it into the mouth
without dribbling. The brown crust on the bottom of the pan is
considered the prize.

Note: This recipe as given is meant to serve 6 persons, but when the
first lot is finished, it is easy enough to make a second lot, especially
if the cheese mixture has been prepared and is waiting in a bowl, ready
to be added. This means that for the two lots, you will need a full
bottle of white wine, to be used only for making the fondue.

FOURTH OF JULY WINE AND CHEESE PARTY

What could be more appropriate on the Fourth than an all-American
tasting of wines and cheeses?

Make it a neighborhood affair, served on the lawn. The tasting
could be in late afternoon or even after dark, with flaming torches to
light up the yard.

For other snacks wanted at the Fourth of July independence celebration, select some that represent unique American contributions to
gastronomy, as do the wines and cheeses named below. For example,

the crispest of potato chips (ones made with real potatoes, not dried potato granules); Pascal celery (a hybrid triumph); cherry tomatoes, the size originally found in the Americas by the earliest Spanish conquistadores; and green peppers, another contribution from the New World to the Old.

And if the wine tasting should end in a barbecue, hamburgers and corn on the cob are equally "native American."

Naturally, the serving tables should be decorated with red, white, and blue bunting, to offset the red, white, and rosé wines and the blue cheeses.

White Wines
Louis Martini Folle Blanche
Boordyblümchen
Paul Masson Emerald Dry

Charles Krug or Ridge Pinot Chardonnay

Rosé Wines
Almadén Grenache Rosé
Chateau Souverain Gamay Rosé

Italian Swiss Colony Vin Rosé

Red Wines
Inglenook Vintage Zinfandel 1968
Christian Brothers Pinot Saint Georges

Bully Hill Baco Noir
Sonoma Vineyards or Fetzger Cabernet Sauvignon

Cheeses
Liederkranz
Brick or fontinella
An aged Monterey jack
Maytag Blue Cheese

Colorado Blackie, Herkimer County, or some other especially fine aged American Cheddar

Buffet Menu
Assorted vegetable relishes
Potato chips, corn chips, pretzel sticks, cheese niblets
Barbecued hamburgers and Sloppy Joes, with buns and assorted hamburger relishes
Corn on the cob

Molded Apple Cheese Salad *(see page 117)*
Tossed Vegetable Salad with Caesar Dressing *(see page 118)*
Assorted cakes and pies contributed by neighborhood cooks participating in the celebration

About the wines: Each is recommended because it is notable for one reason or another in the history of the American wine industry. Folle Blanche is made exclusively by Louis Martini from a grape found growing wild on his Saint Helena vineyard when he first purchased the estate, and though it is a *Vitis vinifera* variety, it has not been definitely identified.

Boordyblümchen, produced in the area bordering the shores of Lake Erie in northern New York, is an example of a wine made from French-American hybrids. Emerald Dry is made from another American hybrid, the Emerald Riesling developed at Davis in California. At least one Pinot Chardonnay should be included, because among American white wines this is considered the finest of all the varietals. Ridge Vineyards, while it is small and its wines may not be widely distributed, is one of the finest of the California wineries. Charles Krug wines are available almost everywhere.

Almadén's Grenache Rosé is included because it was the first of its kind and can be credited with doing much to make rosé wines so popular with Americans. The other two rosés are suggested as samples of how different rosé wines can be, according to the grape variety and method of production.

Of the red wines, all suggested are outstanding wines, each with its own special quality.

It wouldn't be a proper Fourth celebration without at least one Zinfandel, since only in the United States are wines made with this grape variety (though it is now being used for certain blended wines in European wineries). The Pinot Saint Georges is also unique, one of Christian Brothers' most interesting red wines, light and slightly tart.

As for the Cabernet Sauvignon, this is the variety responsible for the California red wines that moved French experts to warn their fellow countrymen that they had better get ready to move over and share their reputation for superiority in viticulture with some of the American vintners. It was also the success of Cabernet Sauvignon as a California wine that sparked the trend now followed in other countries of giving wines varietal names, instead of or in addition to regional names. For the best samples of this great varietal, it is best to choose those of one of the smaller, private wineries, rather than the bigger ones. Besides those named above, look for Louis Martini, Sterling, Oakville, Wente, Concannon, Sebastiani, or Robert Mondavi. Since these need age, look for a 1969 or 1970 vintage, though the Mondavi 1971 is outstanding.

About the cheeses: These, too, have been selected because each deserves an American star. Liederkranz is the finest of the American soft ripened cheeses, an American original with unique flavor. Unfortunately, it is not in wide distribution, and can usually be found only in a cheese specialty shop.

Monterey jack is a California original that at its best is truly beautiful, though the supermarket samples rarely do it justice. Brick is also uniquely American, though, like Liederkranz, not in wide distribution. If it cannot be found, a mild Cheddar might be chosen instead. Maytag blue cheese is growing fast in popularity because it is so delicate and creamy—and the washing machine company is to be congratulated for producing such a fine gourmet product in its curious corporate entry into the field of gastronomy.

Naturally, there must be a sample of aged, flaky Cheddar, and one cut from a big wheel, not the plastic-wrapped "natural Cheddars" of the supermarket. The two named are mere suggestions. Perhaps a local farmer's Cheddar can be found, the type once called "rat cheese," which will be just as noteworthy.

Molded Apple Cheese Salad

    1 three-ounce package lemon-flavored gelatin
    1 cup boiling water
    7 to 10 ice cubes
    1 tablespoon lemon juice
    1½ cups finely chopped apples
    ⅔ cup shredded Swiss cheese
    ¼ cup chopped walnuts

¼ cup diced celery
1 teaspoon grated onion
½ teaspoon salt

Dissolve the gelatin in hot water, then add the ice cubes and stir until the gelatin is thickened, about 3 minutes. Remove any bits of ice not melted.

Sprinkle the lemon juice over the apples, to prevent discoloration, then combine the apples with the cheese, nuts, celery, onion, and salt. Fold into the thickened gelatin and pour into a mold. Chill until very firm.

Unmold on lettuce and serve with a dressing made of equal parts mayonnaise and sour cream, or offer a selection of prepared dressings. *Makes 8 to 10 servings.*

Tossed Vegetable Salad

If more than twenty persons are joining in on this celebration, one molded salad will not be enough. Besides, it seems appropriately American to have at least one big tossed salad.

1 cup shredded red cabbage
1 cup sliced fresh, raw mushrooms
½ green pepper, sliced thin
1 small jar pimientos, drained and sliced
1 small white onion, sliced paper thin and broken into rings
1 cup garlic-flavored croutons
6 to 8 cups torn mixed salad greens
Caesar Salad Dressing

Combine all the ingredients except the dressing in a large wooden bowl. Cover tightly with plastic wrap and keep chilled in the refrigerator until serving time. Toss with a little of the dressing before serving, or serve it from the bowl, letting those who wish another dressing to choose from an assortment. *Makes 8 to 10 salad servings.*

Caesar Salad Dressing

3 large garlic cloves, split
⅓ cup olive oil
3 anchovy fillets, rinsed and crushed
½ teaspoon salt
1 egg, beaten
½ cup freshly grated Parmesan cheese
2 tablespoons red wine vinegar
¼ cup sour cream (optional)

Crush the garlic cloves in a wooden or Pyrex mixing bowl, using a wooden pestle or the back of a wooden spoon until nothing but shreds remain. Remove the shreds (the juice and flavor will remain in the bowl). Rinse the anchovy fillets briefly in warm water to get rid of excess salt, then add to the garlic-flavored bowl and mash to a paste. Beat in the olive oil, a little at a time, then beat in raw egg, salt, then the cheese, and finally the vinegar. (This can all be done in a blender at moderate speed.) If desired, ¼ cup sour cream may be added to make it a cream dressing. *Makes 1 to 1-¼ cups.*

A WINE HARVEST PARTY

For a more bacchanalian salute to the wine god, a rip-roaring fun occasion, why not have a wine harvest celebration? It should be in the fall of the year, September or October.

To provide the real feel of a harvest setting, clusters of grapes might be piled high in fruit bowls or sent spilling from cornucopias (if someone can make these from cardboard or papier-mâché). Background music of Old World folk dances or songs should be played over the stereo, unless you know someone who can furnish live music from an accordion or guitar.

If possible, try to locate a porrón. This won't be easy. If there is a local Italian-American organization, ask its members if they know of someone who has one. Or, if you live in a state that boasts its own wine industry, inquire of the various wineries. A porrón is a drinking vessel that looks something like a carafe but has two long spouts, one long and thin, tapered almost to a point. This has been used since ancient times to pour wine directly into one's mouth in a stream. It's a much more difficult feat than you would think; in fact, only someone with long practice can do it successfully the first time. But in an atmosphere of hilarity, there will be many, men especially, who will try. Be sure to provide bibs, of the kind used for eating lobster.

Another diversion might be the pressing of fresh grapes with bare feet, the original method, used for thousands of years, to extract the must. Probably the biggest drawback here is that it would be difficult to find the proper kind of trough in which to perform the ritual. It could be a small boat, or an old bathtub or big wooden tub rescued from junk yard or city dump, or a trough erected of plywood especially for the occasion. The juice, of course, is likely to splash all over the place and leave a red stain, so the pressing of the grapes should take place on the grass, in a garage, or on a patio covered with a plastic drop cloth. Any grapes can be used, preferably gathered from the trellises of people you know, since buying them for this purpose could run into a lot of money.

The grape pressers must be barefoot and dressed in shorts, and when they step into the "vat," link arms at shoulder height and move back and forth in rhythm, pressing the grapes with their bare feet, in time to appropriate music and with the crowd clapping hands and singing.

Even if accouterments like porrón and vat are impossible to locate or provide, music and decorations can contribute to the atmosphere of celebration.

On such an occasion any kind of glasses will do, and juice glasses are just fine. The wine chosen should be served from gallon or half-gallon jugs, and include both American and imported selections. Those which come in straw-covered bottles are especially appropriate. It is also possible in some localities to obtain barrels of wine, each of which contain approximately five gallons. But unless this is a big crowd, and five gallons will only begin to satisfy their thirst, this would mean only one kind of wine could be served, which is rather spoiling the point.

Vins ordinaires should be chosen, for the most part, rather than premium wines, since this comes under the classification of party rather than tasting. It should also be noted that young wines, from last year's vintage, are those usually served at a wine harvest.

For the cheeses, serve mostly the types that owe their distinctive flavor to the caves or cellars where the original cheeses acquired their flavor-making microorganisms, plus the firmer cheeses that are (or once were) typical of local farm cheeses.

White Wines

Italian Swiss Colony Moselle
Gold Seal Chablis Nature

Cresta Blanca or Widmer Sauterne
Paul Masson Rhine Castle

Rosé Wines

Gallo Pink Chablis
Weibel Classic Vin Rosé
Gold Seal or Great Western (New York) Vin Rosé

Spanish rosé wine (Barcelona or Tarragona), in a straw demijohn

Red Wines

Ruffino or Grifoni Chianti (Italian), in a straw demijohn
Gambarelli & Daviotto Fior de California

Almadén Mountain Red Claret
Wine Growers Guild Burgundy

Cheeses

Port Salut or Oka
"Cave-aged" blue cheese
Young Monterey jack or Swiss

Quarter wheel of well-aged sharp Cheddar
Raclette (see below)

Buffet Menu

To accompany the Raclette, boiled potatoes, sausages, French and rye bread
Anchoïade (see below)
Stuffed Edam (see below)
Thin-sliced salty rye and pumpernickel

Assorted crackers, pretzels, other nibblers
Bowls of grapes and apples
Homemade cookies, such as hermits and oatmeal cookies

About the wines: All suggested are available (in some markets, at least) in half gallons, gallons, magnums, or demijohns. Moselle is a new Italian Swiss Colony white wine; Rhine Castle is a semidry white wine, with more sweetness than the Paul Masson Emerald Dry.

Demijohn jugs of wine covered with straw are suggested because these seem so typical of country wines. If pouring the wine from such big jugs is difficult, transfer them to pitchers—it's the way wine is served at a typical harvest.

Glassware can be of the simplest: punch cups will do, or any small glasses, such as juice glasses. Stemware is not necessary.

About the cheese: Of the cheeses suggested, the most appropriate are those in big wedges or wheels, even if this means having only two big cheeses and perhaps a pâté or two.

Raclette

Raclette is actually the name of an appliance used for melting cheese rather than the cheese itself; the cheese most favored for making the dish known as Raclette in Switzerland goes by the name of mütschli (not to be confused with the breakfast cereal of almost the same name). However, in cheese specialty shops the cheese is more often sold by the name Raclette.

Buy a big wedge of imported Raclette cheese from Switzerland, or use any mild-flavored melting cheese, such as mozzarella or domestic Swiss. It is important to have a thick piece, preferably at least two pounds, otherwise scraping it off as it melts will be difficult.

Raclette stoves, made especially for the purpose, can be purchased in some cheese stores or gourmet shops, but it can be done just as well in a broiler oven or the broiler of your kitchen range. As the top of the cheese becomes soft, scrape off a portion for each serving, transfer to a plate. Forks will be necessary for eating the cheese. Serve with boiled potatoes; mash the melted cheese and potatoes together.

Another way to melt the cheese is to place it on the hearth of the fireplace with a big fire roaring in the fireplace—though this is suitable only for serving in cool weather. In summer, it may be placed next to an outdoor barbecue oven, close enough to the heat of the fire to cause it to melt.

Serve pickles on the side. Hot sausage may or may not be offered as well.

Anchoïade

6 anchovy fillets
4 large or 6 small tomatoes, sliced
3 large garlic cloves, crushed
½ teaspoon dried basil
¼ cup olive oil
Few drops vinegar
1 long, thin loaf French or sourdough bread

Rinse the anchovy fillets in warm water to remove excess salt, then drain and set aside. Cook the tomatoes, garlic, and basil in the oil until the tomatoes are soft but still hold their shape. Add to the drained anchovies and mash to a paste, working in the vinegar.

Slice the bread in half lengthwise and spread the mixture thinly over the cut side of the bread, both halves. Cut the bread into 2-inch pieces, and just before serving, place the bread under the broiler, 3 inches from heat, until lightly toasted. *Makes about 24 individual pieces, depending on the length of the loaf.*

Note: Serve only with red wine; this is too garlicky for white or rosé wine.

Stuffed Edam

1 large (14 ounce) Edam cheese
2 to 3 tablespoons sherry or white wine
¼ cup butter or margarine
¼ cup shelled, salted sunflower seeds or caraway seeds

Slice off the top of the round ball of cheese, then scoop out as much of the cheese from the inside as possible. (This will be easier if the cheese has been at room temperature for at least an hour.) Setting the shell and sliced-off top aside, beat the scooped-out cheese with the wine and butter or margarine until smooth. Work in the seeds, then return to the shell and cover with the sliced-off top. To serve, scoop out the cheese with a spoon or use a butter knife to remove. Spread over thin-sliced salty rye, pumpernickel, or crackers. *Makes 30 to 35 canapé servings.*

A SPARKLING WINE AND CHEESE CELEBRATION TASTING

Sparkling wines have always been popular with Americans. In the hundred years before the shadow of Prohibition fell over the land, more champagnes and sweet wines were produced here than table wines. And while the picture has now changed, sparkling wines are still the favorite for celebrations, and to set out a selection of bubbly wines that have—to make a crude pun— tickled the palates of Americans in the last decade is to realize how many different kinds of sparkling wines are now available for celebrating.

Should a sample of cold duck be on the menu? I'm told that this curious, and to a connoisseur, rather horrible drink no longer retains the popularity of a few years ago—that, in fact, cold duck is rapidly becoming a "dead duck."

The drink originated in Germany, where traditionally it was made up of leftovers after a party. The name, *kalte Ende,* meant "leftovers," but it sounded so much like *kalte Ente,* meaning, literally, "cold duck" in German, that the latter name became popular. In Germany the drink is still served, but usually consists of a mixture of champagne and still white wine, flavored with a spiral of lemon rind. And perhaps this, which is really a champagne punch, is the best kind of cold duck to serve at your celebration. Or you may prefer to make a true champagne punch according to the recipe on page 124.

An appropriate occasion for a tasting of sparkling wines would be an anniversary party, or a college graduation celebration, or some other such special occasion—perhaps a club's final meeting of the year.

The following list of suggested wines is intended to please all tastes. It includes everything from brut, the driest champagne, to the very sweet bubblies, white, pink, and red. Purposely several European sparkling wines have been included, for comparison.

Bland, light, or delicate cheeses are always best with champagnes. Besides the cheese, thin unflavored wafers, macaroons, and Jordan almonds might be offered, as well as other light cheesy hors d'oeuvres.

For a serious tasting of champagnes, the tall, tulip-shaped champagne glasses are preferable, though the shallow "saucer" glasses are more traditional. If rented for the occasion, any rental firm company asked to furnish champagne glasses is bound to supply the saucer shape. If it's a rather small group, to supplement a home supply of champagne glasses and standard eight-ounce tulip shape stemware, sherbet glasses can be used if necessary.

Wines

Asti Extra Dry California Champagne

Schramsberg or Korbel Brut Champagne, or Sonoma Vineyards Sparkling Pinot Chardonnay

Cordorniu Espumante Sec (Spanish)

Gold Seal or Taylor Pink Champagne, or Mirassou Sparkling Gamay Beaujolais

Asti Spumante (Italian)

Boyer Brut or Vouvray Crémant

Almadén Sparkling Burgundy
Champagne Punch (see page 124)

Cheese

Crema Danica
Gourmandise
Havarti or Dobo Danish Brick

Natural Gruyère
Almond-Crusted Camembert (see page 124)

Buffet Menu

Crab Quiche (see page 125)
Thin crackers or wafers

Jordan almonds
Mints

About the wines: In Europe, no sparkling wines except those from the Champagne wine district can legally be called "champagne," by mutual agreement among Continental wine producers, though locally, in each wine country, they are always referred to as champagnes nevertheless.

The Spanish name for sparkling wines is *espumante;* the Italian is *spumante.* The Spanish champagne suggested is one of Spain's best, and what is classified as *sec* in Spain is somewhat drier than the American champagnes with this label. Asti Spumante is, however, a sweet wine, and therefore should be among the last to be tasted.

While the French Champagnes are known throughout the world as superb wines, beautifully balanced, and with exquisite bouquet, there are other French sparkling wines made by the champagne process that are also very, very good and much less costly. Some cost less than American champagnes of comparable quality. Boyer Brut, produced in the region of the French Pyrénées, an unclassified wine district, is such a sparkling wine. Vouvray is the sparkling version of the semisweet white wine of the Loire, and when produced by the champagne process (the label will specify), is like a champagne.

Whatever sparkling wines are decided upon, there should be at least one champagne from California and one from New York State for comparison. Most of the New York State champagnes are still made primarily with *Vitis labrusca* grapes blended with hybrid varieties; an exception is Gold Seal's Charles Fournier Blanc de Blancs champagne made primarily with Pinot Chardonnay grapes. In the Champagne district of France, the wine is made from a blend of Pinot Chardonnay and Pino Noir grapes; these two varieties also form the basis of the finest of California champagnes, though Mirassou recently introduced one made with Pinot Blanc and Chenin Blanc grapes. Most renowned of the California champagne makers are Schramsberg and Korbel.

Wine connoisseurs nearly always prefer a brut champagne, the driest of all (the word means natural, or without sugar). Any American champagne called Blanc de Blancs means a dry champagne, though it may have a trace more sweetness than those labeled brut. While the French word *sec* means literally "dry," in fact the champagnes so labeled are somewhat sweeter than the brut, and may be decidely sweet (depending on the maker). One test of a fine champagne lies in the bubbles; they should be very tiny and last a long time. If the champagne is served in a tall tulip-shaped champagne glass they will last longer than in the saucer shape.

When a champagne bottle carries the designation *methode champenoise* it means the wine was fermented in the bottle, though today most champagnes are fermented in steel, in the tanks, then transferred to the bottles for capping and aging. The *methode champenoise* is generally considered preferable both for delicacy and balance of taste and for greater bouquet, but such champagnes will also be considerably more costly.

For variety, you will probably want to serve a sparkling pink wine, perhaps a sparkling burgundy (red). Mirassou's Sparkling Gamay Beaujolais is more a pink than a red wine. For a sweet sparkling wine, the Italian Asti Spumante is very highly regarded—or you may choose a dulce champagne. There is also a Sparkling Catawba and, of course, cold duck. These last won't be to everyone's taste—but then neither is brut champagne.

How much to buy? As for other tastings, half a bottle of wine per person is ample, and could be more than ample. Avoid opening more than will be needed, because once opened, champagne, or any other sparkling wine, must be finished that day. It's no good when it's a "dead duck."

About the cheese: The same cheeses suitable for serving with white wine are best with champagne and other sparkling wines. All must be delicate and fairly bland in flavor.

It is not necessary to add a pastry such as the Crab Quiche, a recipe for which follows, unless the host feels it would make the appetizer table seem more interesting. The quiche can be served cold, but the last stage of baking should be the morning of the day of the tasting; otherwise, the pastry may become soggy.

Champagne Punch

> 3 tablespoons granulated sugar
> 2 cups water
> ½ cup orange juice
> 2 tablespoons lemon juice
> ¼ cup peach syrup (from canned peaches)
> ¼ cup light rum
> ⅒ bottle or 1¾ cups dry white wine
> Strawberry halves, maraschino cherries, and orange slices for garnish
> 1 magnum brut or dry champagne

Combine the sugar and water in a saucepan and bring to a boil; simmer until the sugar is completely dissolved, then cool. Add the orange juice, lemon juice, peach syrup, and rum. Add the white wine to the fruit juice and rum mixture and pour over blocks of ice in a punch bowl (see note below). Add the fruit for garnish. Just before serving, open champagne and add to the punch bowl. *Makes about 25 punch cup servings.*

Note: To make blocks of ice, fill two empty half-gallon milk cartons with water and freeze. (Be sure to rinse out the cartons thoroughly first.) Within the last half hour before the guests are due, unmold the ice by pulling off the waxed cartons and place in the punch bowl.

Almond-crusted Camembert Pâté

> 1 eight-ounce wheel of Camembert
> ¼ cup medium-sweet or cream sherry

4 tablespoons butter or margarine

4 ounces (½ package) farmer cheese; or ½ cup creamed cottage cheese

½ cup slivered, toasted almonds (or minced pecans, or shelled salted sunflower seeds)

Slice off white crust of Camembert with small sharp knife. Cut cheese in small pieces, soak in sherry at room temperature overnight. Next day, beat by hand or in blender, adding butter or margarine and farmer or cottage cheese with blender in motion, until very smooth. Line a small (2-cup) mold with plastic wrap, spoon in cheese mixture, pack down tightly. Chill until firm, about 2 hours. Remove from mold, pull off plastic and press nuts thickly over surface. Return to refrigerator until 1 hour before serving. Camembert flavor predominates but mixture is more delicate and buttery than Camembert by itself. Also, sherry in cheese mixture helps cheese to keep fresh longer. Delicious with any wine but particularly white or rosé. *Makes 1½ cups.*

Crab Quiche

Pastry for a 1-crust pie

1 egg white

¾ to 1 cup finely flaked crabmeat, all gristle removed

1 cup shredded Swiss cheese

¼ cup freshly grated Parmesan cheese

2 cups light cream or dairy half-and-half

2 eggs, well beaten

½ teaspoon salt

1 teaspoon freeze-dried chives

Pinch cayenne or curry powder

Prepare the pastry and roll out very thin, then use it to fill a 9-inch pie pan, fluting the edges so that the crust stands up above the pan. Brush the bottom of the crust with egg white to prevent the filling from soaking into the pastry, then chill in the freezer while preparing the filling.

Combine the finely flaked crabmeat with the cheeses and blend well, then add the remaining ingredients. Pour into the chilled pastry shell and bake in a preheated 425-degree oven for 10 minutes, then lower the heat to 325 degrees for 30 minutes, or until a knife inserted in the center comes out clean. Cut in thin wedges for appetizer servings. *Makes 10 servings.*

Note: Since this recipe makes only 10 servings, if you are expecting 20 guests, this means making at least two separate quiches. However, all can be made ahead, baked for a total of no more than 30 minutes, then wrapped in plastic and frozen until needed. Complete the baking by starting in a cold oven set at 325 degrees for 20 minutes, or until the knife comes out clean.

How to open a champagne bottle: First make sure each bottle is thoroughly chilled—otherwise all the wine will foam over, and you might even have an explosion. When well chilled and ready to serve, remove the wire, next the foil, and now holding the bottle at a 45 degree angle, slowly, slowly push the cork with your thumbs, first on one side, then another. In Europe, it's considered a disgrace to allow the cork to pop. Here that's considered the fun of the whole thing. But in any case, have glasses ready and handy to serve, or there's no telling where the foam will spurt to.

A TASTING OF
DESSERT WINES AND CHEESES

Dessert wines are in a different class and serve a different function from table wines, and should be sampled at a separate tasting. This is a good idea for an evening gathering, after dinner.

An interesting tasting would be to compare famous European sweet wines with American dessert wines, especially those of the same name —or made from the same grape varieties.

Among the world's most highly prized sweet unfortified wines are the Spätlese, Auslese and Trockenbeerenauslese of Germany, the Sauternes of France, and Hungary's Tokaj wines.

The German word *Spätlese* means "late picked," and wines that have this word on the label will always be sweeter, because the grapes left longer on the vine develop more natural sugar. *Trockenbeerenauslese*, which means "dried berry selected," indicates that for these the grapes were allowed to dry on the vine, and then each was individually picked, sometimes only half a dozen grapes from each bunch. Because of labor costs, there are very few of the Trockenbeerenauslese wines available, and if found they are bound to be of astronomical price.

Like the Sauternes of France, the late-picked Rhine grapes have usually been touched by *Botrytis cinerea*, or "noble rot," the fungus that causes the grape skins to shrivel, and not only concentrates the sugar content, making the wines sweeter, but gives the wine an indefinable quality, a peculiarly rich fragrance and bouquet. In recent years this same fungus has begun to appear in California vineyards, but only two or three times in a decade.

The Hungarian wines called Tokaj all come from a carefully guarded wine region with unique soil conditions. Catherine the Great of Russia is said to have furnished a special unit of her guards to protect the vineyards furnishing her with her own supply of Tokaj each year. The wines have been famous since the Middle Ages, when Crusaders crossing Europe to reach the Holy Land, first encountered them. The individually picked aszú grapes (the word aszú connotes in Hungarian the same thing as Trockenbeerenauslese) are placed in canvas bags to be crushed, then this rich concentrate is blended with wine from grapes picked somewhat earlier. Prize bottles of Tokaj carry a Puttonyos rating, the word *puttonyos* meaning "bags," and indicating how many bags of the rich aszú concentrate have gone into each lot of wine. If it is a 5 Puttonyos Tokaj, it is an especially rich, sweet wine. The flavor and bouquet of Tokaj cannot be compared to that of any other wine in the world; it is truly unique. Sometimes the aszú grapes are picked after snow lies on the ground around them, and this, too, is said to contribute to their unique flavor.

The brandy-fortified sweet wines are still different. The greatest of these include the vintage and crusted ports, the vintage Malmsey Madeiras, and the solera-blended and aged cream sherries of Spain. The method of making each of these has been described earlier. There are some American cream sherries that compare very well with the Spanish, but we have nothing as yet in the same class as a vintage port. Once upon a time, every well-to-do English family laid down a bottle of vintage port upon the birth of a son, the bottle to be opened upon his twenty-first birthday and not a day sooner. The high price of vintage port today has changed this, nor is port regarded with quite the same awe as formerly. Nevertheless, this is a connoisseur's wine, one that should be experienced at least once in a lifetime.

As for price, even when these wines are very expensive, their life is not as limited as that of table wines, and the fortified wines remain drinkable almost indefinitely because of the brandy content. Very small servings need be poured; one bottle goes a very long way.

When a sweet wine is poured, and the glass tilted, "tears" or "legs," as they are variously called in different countries, can be seen to run down the side of the glass. Twisting the glass to see this syrupy richness is part of the ritual of sampling a dessert wine.

Two kinds of tastings of dessert wines are suggested: one for a mixed group of acquaintances not passionately interested in wine lore and therefore less likely to be impressed with the richness of a costly 5 Puttonyo Tokaj or a vintage port, the second for people who do have a lively curiosity about the world's truly great sweet wines.

The cheeses for any dessert wine tasting should be delicate in flavor, including both light and firmer types, but the latter with a buttery rather than hard texture. Cookies, cheesecake, and sponge cake may also be offered.

DESSERT WINE AND CHEESE TASTING (FOR MIXED GROUP)

Wines
Christian Brothers Château La Salle
Charles Krug Moscato di Canelli
Est! Est!! Est!!! (Italian)

Croft or Sandeman Tawny Port
Almadén Tinta Ruby Port
Manischewitz Kosher Wine

Cheese
Jack in Port *(see page 128)*

Crème de Gruyère
Gervais or Petite Suisse *(see page 128)*

Accompaniments
Easy Coconut Macaroons *(see page 128)*

Brandied Fruit Cake *(see page 129)*
Jacob's biscuits for cheese

About the wines: Both imported and American wines have been suggested, though should the imported wines seem too costly for the type of party being given, they could be omitted and only the four dessert wines offered, with the possible addition of a cream sherry.

The Italian wine Est! Est!! Est!!! may be of interest for its name alone. It is said that a sixteenth-century cardinal, about to make a tour of his parishes, sent his valet ahead to test the wine served at each inn. The valet was instructed that each time he found an inn that served good wine, to chalk *Est!* ("this is it") on the door. At the town of Montefiascone, he found wine so exalting that he scratched *Est! Est!! Est!!!* on the door—and the name stuck to the local wine, a golden, smooth, luscious dessert wine that goes beautifully with sponge cake or fruit cake.

Both Croft and Sandeman are famous shippers' names in Oporto, where for many centuries the port wine business has been dominated by Englishmen. A fine tawny acquires its color only with age, and also becomes less sweet as it ages in the bottle. But because it is less sweet, it should be tasted before a ruby port.

Some of the American wines called "port" are very sad imitations of the fortified wine from Portugal, but now some of the premium wineries are importing grape varieties from Portugal and bottle aging their wines several years before placing them on the market; such ports will compare more favorably with those made with wines from the spectacular Douro wine region.

Petit Suisse

1 eight-ounce package cream or farmer cheese, softened
1 tablespoon confectioners' sugar
2 tablespoons heavy cream or sour cream
Vanilla wafers or bland crackers
Strawberry or red raspberry jam

Beat the cheese until fluffy, then gradually beat in the sugar and cream. Pack into small bowl and chill. Spread vanilla wafers with jam and top with the cheese spread, or place the bowl of chilled cheese on a platter with a small bowl of jam with vanilla wafers or bland crackers on the side, to be spread as served (as for cocktail pâtés on crackers). *Makes about 1 cup.*

Jack in Port

½ pound well-aged Monterey jack or 1 eight-ounce stick **Caljak,** grated
⅓ cup tawny or ruby port
⅓ cup light cream

Put all the ingredients in the blender and whir until smooth, about 40 seconds. Turn into a serving bowl and chill overnight, covered. Remove 30 minutes before serving. Serve on Bremner crackers. *Makes a little more than 1 cup.*

Easy Coconut Macaroons

2 cups finely grated coconut
¾ cup sweetened condensed milk
Dash salt
1 teaspoon vanilla extract
¼ teaspoon almond extract

Combine all the ingredients and let stand for 2 to 3 minutes. Preheat the oven to 325 degrees. Spread brown paper on a baking sheet; grease the paper. Drop the coconut mixture by teaspoonfuls 1 inch apart on the brown paper, then flatten with the back of a spoon. Bake until golden, about 25 minutes. Remove immediately from the baking sheet with a spatula and cool on a flat surface covered with waxed paper. Store in a covered container. *Makes about 3 dozen.*

Brandied Fruit Cake

Buy a good quality fruit cake, or make one from a favorite recipe. Sprinkle liberally with brandy on all sides, then wrap in brandy-soaked cheesecloth, overwrap in foil, and place in the refrigerator or a cool, dark place to ripen for at least a week.

Note: The cake will slice more easily if refrigerator cold, and a well-sharpened, thin-bladed knife is used.

A GOURMET DESSERT WINE TASTING

American Wines

Taylor Sauterne

Château Wente or Oakville Sauvignon Fleur 1972

Mirassou Spätlese Riesling 1972

Paul Masson Tinta Madeira Port

Imported Wines

Sauternes or Barsac from the Bordeaux wine region

Schloss Vollrads or Rudesheimer Riesling Spätlese

Hungarian Tokaj, 4 or 5 puttonyos

Cockburn Crusted or Vintage Port

Cheese

A runny-soft Brie

Caerphilly

Taleggio

Stilton

Accompaniments

Bland unsalted or lightly salted crackers

Apple Cheese Pâté Spread *(see page 130)*

Orange Spritz Cookies *(see page 130)*

Classic Cheesecake *(see page 130)*

About the wines: The Taylor Sauterne is suggested as a contrast to the French Sauternes (or Barsac) and as an example of how different the American wines called "sauterne" are from the French. More nearly like the French Sauternes is the Château Wente, made with Sémillon grapes, for true Sauternes is made with approximately two-thirds Sémillon and one-third Sauvignon Blanc grapes. But the Oakville Sauvignon Fleur is also in the same class, as a dessert wine with superb bouquet and luscious flavor.

The Masson Tinta Madeira port is a ruby port; the name Tinta Madeira refers to the grape variety, it has nothing to do with the island of Madeira. Masson also has a Souzão port, made with a still different grape variety.

All the imported wines suggested above are epicurean and costly. But the only way to understand why they are costly is to sample them at a tasting. Schloss Vollrads and Rudesheimer are two vineyard regions in the Rheingau where the heaviest and fruitiest of German white wines are produced, and a Spätlese or an Auslese from this region is bound to be very special, especially if from one of the better vintage years.

It is not necessary to know any brand name or shipper's name for a Tokaj, because any classed as a 4 or 5 puttonyos Tokaj will be worth the price. For educational reasons, you might want to pick up a bottle of inexpensive American Tokay wine, just to see what eons apart these two wines are.

Expect the price of a crusted or vintage port to be high, if you can locate one. But in comparison with the prices now charged for vintage French château wines, the cost of a crusted port can seem quite reasonable, especially as the fortified wine will last so long after opening.

Apple Cheese Pâté

½ cup creamed cottage cheese or ricotta
¼ cup crumbled blue cheese
¼ cup feta or goat cheese
½ cup finely chopped apples
2 tablespoons cream sherry or brandy

Combine the ingredients in the order given and beat until well blended. Serve on Triscuits. *Makes 1-½ cups.*

Note: This goes well with almost any wine—white, dry, or sweet, or port—and also with red table wine.

Orange Spritz Cookies

These should be made with a cookie press, but if you don't have one, chill the dough thoroughly, then roll out between wax paper and cut into circles or other shapes with cookie cutters.

2½ cups sifted all-purpose flour
¼ teaspoon salt
¼ teaspoon baking soda
1 cup softened butter or margarine
½ cup granulated sugar
½ cup brown sugar, firmly packed
1 tablespoon orange juice
1 tablespoon grated orange rind
1 egg

Sift together the flour, salt, and baking soda and set aside. Cream together the butter and sugars until light and fluffy, then beat in the orange juice, grated rind, and egg, then the flour mixture. When well blended, place about one-quarter of the dough at a time in a cookie press and press out onto an ungreased baking sheet. (Keep the cookies small, for they will spread out with baking.) Bake in a preheated 375-degree oven for 10 to 12 minutes, or until delicately browned. Repeat until all are baked. Keep stored in an airtight container. *Makes about 6 dozen.*

Classic Cheesecake

2 tablespoons softened butter, approximately
1 six-ounce package zweiback
¼ cup confectioners' sugar

6 tablespoons melted butter
1½ pounds (3 eight-ounce packages) cream cheese or farmer cheese, softened
2 tablespoons cornstarch, or 4 tablespoons flour
1 cup granulated sugar
¼ teaspoon salt
4 eggs, separated, plus 2 egg yolks
1 cup heavy cream
Juice and grated rind of 1 lemon

First rub the bottom and sides of a 9-inch springform pan, or a 10-inch pan with removable bottom, with the softened butter. Crush the zwieback to make 2½ cups crumbs. Sprinkle as many crumbs as needed over the bottom and 2 inches up the sides of the pan, pressing them into the butter. Blend the remaining crumbs with the confectioners' sugar and melted butter and set aside.

Beat the softened cream or farmer cheese vigorously until light and fluffy. Add the cornstarch, flour, sugar, salt, and the 6 egg yolks (keeping aside the 4 egg whites). When well blended, add the heavy cream, then the lemon juice and rind, and continue to beat until very smooth. Whip the reserved egg whites until stiff; fold into the cheese mixture.

Pour the cheese mixture over the crumbs in the pan. Spread or sprinkle the reserved buttered crumb mixture over the filling and bake in a 325-degree oven for 1 hour, then turn off the oven and let the cheesecake remain in the warm oven for an additional 30 minutes. Remove and let cool in the pan. When completely cool, remove the cheesecake from the pan by loosening around the sides with a spatula, then take off the upper part of the pan, and with the spatula, loosen the cake from the bottom. *Makes 16 to 18 small but rich servings.*

A BLIND TASTING CONTEST

As different from the intimate exploratory tastings suggested earlier, this would be a serious effort to guess which is the American, which the imported wine made from the same grape varieties. A similar blind tasting of cheeses could be carried out afterward.

Instead of simply covering over the labels on the bottles, for this tasting the participants might actually be blindfolded, brought forward one at a time, and handed first one glass containing sample X, then a second glass containing sample Y, then while still blindfolded, asked to identify the wines as to color, type, and country of origin. Someone, an assistant to the host, must be delegated to write down the guesses under each participant's name.

It is astonishing how often the blindfolded tasters will even guess wrong about the color of the wine, let alone the type and origin.

Naturally, those who have not yet tasted the samples should remain in another room and the results not be announced until everyone has had a go at it. The number of wines tasted should be limited—the following list suggests a considerable number from which to choose, but probably no more than four pairs or eight wines should be offered. After the blindfolded contest, the participants should be encouraged to return to the scene, have a look at the labels on the bottles from which the samples were poured, and take another, unblindfolded taste.

The same method would be used for cheese: first a small nibble of one, then a nibble of a second cheese of the same general type, but of different origin. Mix up the order, of course: that is, the first sample may be an American cheese and the second comparative nibble an imported one, but next time around, make the first nibble an imported cheese, the second an American, taking care to reverse the pattern frequently so that the participants won't be tipped off too easily as to which is which.

The following are only suggestions. If the particular wineries suggested are not represented in your local liquor store, look for other varietals of the same name. But be sure to make it a cross section of both lesser and finer wines.

WINE PAIRING POSSIBILITIES

In almost every one of the following, the American wine is either in the same generic classification, or made with the same varietal grapes, as the European counterpart.

American	Imported
White wines	
Sebastiani Gewürztraminer	Alsatian or German Gewürztraminer
Beaulieu Vineyards (BV) Pinot Chardonnay	Chablis or Pinot Chardonnay from Burgundy
Simi Fumé Blanc	Pouilly-Fumé (Loire)
Mirassou White Burgundy	Pouilly-Fuissé (Burgundy)
Widmer New York State Riesling Spätlese	Liebfraumilch (Rhine valley)
Rosé wines	
Boordy Rosé	Mateus Rosé
Concannon Zinfandel Rosé	Rosé d'Anjou (Loire)
Buena Vista Grenache Rosé	Tavel Rosé (Côtes du Rhône)
Red wines	
Gallo or Italian Swiss Colony Chianti	Ruffino Chianti
Paisano Burgundy	Age Red Rioja
Almadén Mountain Claret	Château des Garandières (Bordeaux)
Robert Mondavi Pinot Noir 1971	Mercurey 1969 (Burgundy)
Ridge Zinfandel 1972	Bolla Valpolicella (Italian)
Louis Martini Cabernet Sauvignon 1968 or 1969	Saint-Julien or Cabernet Merlot 1971 (Bordeaux)
Wente Petite-Sirah	Châteauneuf-du-Pape or Côtes du Rhône

CHEESE PAIRING POSSIBILITIES

American	Imported
Kraft Provolone	Italian Provolone
Borden's Camembert	French Camembert
Liederkranz	Reblochou or Port Salut

American Muenster	Muenster from Alsace or
American Brick	Germany
Sugarbush Stiltonbleu	Dofo Danish Brick
Swiss from Wisconsin or Ohio	Genuine English Stilton
Asiago made in New York State	Switzerland Swiss (Emmentaler)
Maytag Blue Cheese	Asiago from Italy
Herkimer County Cheddar	Mycella (from Denmark)
(or other well-aged Cheddar)	Dunlop (Scottish Cheddar)

As the contestants will note, in some cases the American wine or cheese will draw a higher score than (or at least be preferred to) the imported—and in other cases, vice versa. It will also be instructive to learn how completely different in flavor and texture an American wine or cheese may be from the product of the same name originating in another country.

It is not necessary to serve other foods than the cheese for this tasting—except, of course, French or sourdough bread and appropriate bland crackers.

Nor does a contest need prizes. The participants will be rewarded sufficiently in learning how close they come to guessing right when blindfolds force them to depend entirely on taste buds and olfactory senses for identification.

QUIZ CONTESTS

The final meeting of the season for your own little wine club might feature an "examination" something like the following. For this, of course, there must be prizes offered to those who come out with the highest scores, then afterwards, a tasting of some new wines and cheeses—some that haven't been on the tasting agenda earlier in the year. The wines can be white, rosé, or red, new varietals, or inexpensive imported wines that someone has recently come across, to be tasted in comparison with American wines in the same category.

No need to fear about running out of new wines, or new cheeses, to try. Just run your eyes over the selection in cheese specialty shops, and on the shelves of liquor stores that specialize in wine, and you are bound to come upon something you haven't heard of before. We all do, constantly.

True or False

1. Johannisberg Riesling is the name of a famous South African wine.
   True_____ False_____
2. All Burgundies are red. True_____ False_____
3. The chief difference between white and red wines is the length of time that grape skins are left in the pressed juice.
   True_____ False_____
4. Zinfandel is a native American grape. True_____ False_____
5. Rosé wines are so called because originally they were made with roses. True_____ False_____
6. Both wine and cheese are products of natural fermentation.
   True_____ False_____
7. Some rosé wines are made simply by blending together red and white wines. True_____ False_____

8. Brie cheese is made in the Champagne district of France.
True_____ False_____

9. The best place for growing wine grapes is one with a year-round hot climate and very little rainfall. True_____ False_____

10. There are more than eighty kinds of cheese classified as Cheddars. True_____ False_____

11. Normally even a young wine is not ready to drink until the next year after the harvest. True_____ False_____

12. Aging a wine always improves it. True_____ False_____

13. Sharp cheeses go best with red wines. True_____ False_____

14. Rosé wine goes well with any cheese. True_____ False_____

15. "Must" is another name for the very fine sediment that sometimes makes a wine appear cloudy. True_____ False_____

16. Sediment in a wine spoils its flavor. True_____ False_____

17. Caciocavallo is called the "horse cheese" because it used to be fed to horses. True_____ False_____

18. When Gorgonzola is brown around the edges, that is a sign that it is reaching a stage of overripeness. True_____ False_____

Multiple Choice

1. Liederkranz cheese was created by
   (a) Bismarck.
   (b) Metternich, the Austrian statesman and gourmet.
   (c) A Minnesota farmer.
   (d) A New York delicatessen man.

2. The first people to put up wine in glass bottles were
   (a) Monks in medieval France.
   (b) the Romans.
   (c) British vintners in Portugal.
   (d) French immigrants in California during Gold Rush days.

3. When the vintage year is given on a wine label, it means
   (a) the wine is superior.
   (b) that was the year the wine was bottled.
   (c) the wine is made entirely of grapes harvested that year.
   (d) the bottle should not be opened for ten years after that date.

4. A varietal wine
   (a) is made with a variety of grapes.
   (b) is always an American wine.
   (c) will go well with many different dishes.
   (d) is named for the principal grape variety with which it is made.

5. Most red wines should be served at room temperature because
   (a) they will have clearer color.
   (b) their bouquet can be better appreciated.
   (c) they taste better with hot food.
   (d) it's a traditional custom.

6. The phrase "mountain wine" on a label most often means
   (a) the grapes come from a high mountain slope.
   (b) it's a premium wine.
   (c) the opposite of a valley wine.
   (d) the vintner judges it to be somewhat better than his generic or jug wines.

7. The reason for storing wine bottles on their sides is
   (a) to keep the cork moist.
   (b) to save storage space.
   (c) because the wine ages better this way.
   (d) because the bottles look so nice in a wine rack.

8. The reason some cheeses are softer than others is because
   (a) the milk was fresher.
   (b) an enzyme in the cheese prevented it from getting hard.
   (c) less of the whey was extracted from the curd.
   (d) the cheese was ripened in a warm place.

9. Monterey jack gets its name from
   (a) a famous gambler known by that name in early California.
   (b) its origin in or near the town of Monterey, California.
   (c) the type of mold in which it is shaped.
   (d) being the favorite cheese of a California gourmet known as jack.

10. The bubbles in champagne are due to
    (a) the kind of cork used as a stopper.
    (b) the special variety of grapes used.
    (c) added carbon dioxide.
    (d) a second fermentation after the wine is bottled.

Complete the Following Sentences

1. Blue cheese gets its colored veining from_____.
2. Cabernet Sauvignon is a grape variety which originated in_____
   _____.
3. When a wine bottle has a screw cap it usually means the wine
   _____.
4. The best kind of cracker for tasting cheese is_____.
5. The name of England's most famous cheese is_____.
6. Beaujolais is a wine from the_____region of France.
7. The wine region known as Naples Valley is located in_____.
8. Sherry wine originated in_____.
9. The largest wine company in the world is_____.
10. The reason red wines generally age better and live longer than
    white is_____.
11. One of the greatest American wine connoisseurs was_____.
12. In 1850 the American state that had the most flourishing wine
    industry was_____.
13. Today the state that leads all others in cheese production is
    _____.
14. Montrachet is the name of both a cheese and a wine produced in
    _____.
15. France is particularly noted for its_____cheeses.
16. The Hungarian term puttonyo, applied to Tokaj wine, means
    _____.

If you have read this book from start to finish, the answers to all
the above will be easy for you. And if all those to whom the quiz is to
be administered have read the book, it won't be much of a contest. But
if by this time you have become a real expert, it shouldn't be too hard
to make up other true-false and multiple-choice questions, and to
figure out even better "complete this sentence" teasers than the ones
suggested above.

But just in case some of them stump you, here are the answers:

True or False

1. False	10. True
2. False	11. True
3. True	12. False
4. False	13. True
5. False	14. False
6. True	15. False
7. True	16. False
8. True	17. False
9. False	18. True

Multiple Choice

1. (d)	6. (d)
2. (c)	7. (a)
3. (c)	8. (c)
4. (d)	9. (b)
5. (b)	10. (d)

Complete the Following Sentences

1. a microorganism
2. the Bordeaux wine region
3. has been pasteurized
4. bland unsalted
5. Stilton
6. Burgundy
7. New York State
8. Spain
9. Gallo
10. because of the tannin content
11. Thomas Jefferson
12. Ohio
13. Wisconsin
14. the Burgundy region of France
15. soft ripened
16. "bags," meaning the number of bags of aszú concentrate in each lot of wine

AGE CHART

Some wines are best drunk young, some do not reach their peak until after several years of aging. The following is a very general guide; it should be kept in mind that wines of one vintage year will develop sooner, and probably peak sooner than those of another vintage, and conversely, some vintages will enjoy a far longer life than others.

Wine (general classification)	Tends to be best at vintage age . . .
Rosé wines (all)	1 to 1½ years
Generic white wines (chablis, Rhine, sauterne)	1 to 1½ years
Chenin Blanc, Gewürtztraminer, Sylvaner, Emerald or Grey Riesling, French Colombard, Vouvray, most dry white wines	1 to 3 years
Beaujolais, Gamay Beaujolais	2 years
Pinot Chardonnay, Chablis (French), Pouilly-Fuissé, White Graves	2 to 4 years

Johannisberg Riesling, including wines of Mosel and Rhineland	2 to 4 years, some much longer
Generic red wines (burgundy, claret, chianti)	1 to 3 years, depending on the vintner and what grapes have been used in blending
Zinfandel, Ruby Cabernet, Italian Chianti, Corbières (French)	2 to 5 years
Pinot Noir, Barbera, Barolo (Italian)	4 to 10 years
Cabernet Sauvignon, Bordeaux reds, French red Burgundies, Châteauneuf-du-Pape, Petite Sirah	5 to 12 years
Sauternes (French), Montrachet, Tokaj (Hungarian), Trocken-beerenauslese, most sweet white wines	2 to 6 years, some much longer
Port, other fortified semisweet to sweet dessert wines	3 to 12 years or longer

As sherry is a blend of aged and younger wines, it has no vintage age.

WINE-CHEESE AFFINITY CHART

Wine	Cheese
Sherry	Mild to delicately piquant, such as Swiss, Caerphilly, aged jack, Esrom, French goat cheese, Camembert
Vermouths	Sharp, peppery or seeded cheeses, including sharp Cheddar and blue cheese
Dry white wines	Only mild, delicate-flavored, such as Brie, American Muenster, Swiss, Gruyère, fontina, brick, Crema Danica, grape cheese, Havarti
Rosé wines	Only the blandest, creamiest, such as a young jack, Telemi, cream cheese balls, buttery pâtés
Light red wines	Sharper and more pungent than for white wines but more bland than cheeses for robust reds: medium sharp Cheddar, blends of blue cheese, goat cheese, feta, provolone, etc.
Robust reds	Stilton, Roquefort, sharp well-aged Cheddar, Camembert, Port Salut, fontinelli, goat cheeses—all cheeses go well with robust reds, but the above

	are only good with reds, not with other wines.
Demisweet to sweet wines	Soft delicate dessert cheeses, cream cheese, cheesecake, Jarlsberg, natural Gruyère
Sparkling wines	See dry white wines
Port	Same as for other sweet wines, but a tawny port also goes well with Stilton or a young creamy Gorgonzola

SAMPLE SCORING SHEETS

The following is the simplest way to score wines. Give each taster one of the following. Labels may or may not be covered up.

My favorite of the whites was #_____.

My favorite of the reds was #_____.

I found the_____wine to be (mark one): *

⎯⎯⎯ pleasant

⎯⎯⎯ exceptionally nice

⎯⎯⎯ terrible

*(If there is just one of a kind, such as one rosé, or one sherry, or one dessert wine.)

Put out three bottles of red wine, the labels of each carefully covered. Two will be identical bottles of a vintage wine, but one will have been opened at least 1 hour in advance, the other only 5 minutes before serving. The third bottle will be of a lighter wine, or one of lesser quality. Tasters are to guess the identity of each.

	Type or classification	Country of origin	Preference (and why)
# 1			
# 2			
# 3			

SAMPLE SCORING SHEETS

White Wine Tasting: Set out three or four bottles of white wine, each with the label carefully covered over; ask tasters to identify and give preference.

	Dry, semidry, sweet	Country or region of origin	Bouquet	Preference (and why)
# 1				
# 2				
# 3				
# 4				

Rating Test: Samples may include white, rosé, red wines, and variation from very dry to semisweet or sweet.

	Bouquet	First Taste	Aftertaste	Preference (and why)
# 1				
# 2				
# 3				
# 4				
# 5				
# 6				
# 7				
# 8				

INDEX